Copyright 2019
All rights reserved.
Printed in the United States of America

First Edition

The contents of this book are the property of Brown Technical Publications, Inc. All rights reserved. part of this book covered by the copyright hereon may be reproduced, transmitted, stored or used in any form or by any means, graphic, electronic or mechanical, including, but not limited to, photocopying, recording, scanning, digitizing, Web distribution, information networks or by any information storage and retrieval systems, except as permitted under Section 107 or 108 of the 1976 United States Copyright Act, without the prior written permission of the publisher.

While every precaution has been taken in preparation of this book, the author and publisher assumes no responsibility for errors or omissions. Neither is any liability assumed from the use of the information contained herein. The reader is expressly warned to consider and adopt all safety precautions and to avoid all potential hazards. The publisher and author make no representations or warranties of any kind, nor are any such representations implied with respect to the material set forth here. The publisher and author shall not be liable for any special, consequently, or exemplary damages resulting, in whole or part, from the reader's use of, or reliance upon, this material.

Author: One Exam Prep (1-877-804-3959)
www.1examprep.com

ABOUT 1 EXAM PREP

1 EXAM PREP TAKES PRIDE IN BEING THE MOST EFFECTIVE AND EFFICIENT EXAM PREPARATION SCHOOL IN THE INDUSTRY.

All of our Classes and Exam Prep Material is available 24 Hours a Day online when you purchase a online course at www.1examprep.com or call 1-877-804-3959
Access the information whenever and as often as you need.

- No Classrooms
- No Time Schedules
- No Pressure

We provide the TOOLS for YOU to be SUCCESSFUL on YOUR schedule, not ours!
ALL of the Information you need is available at ONE LOW PRICE!

We provide you with exactly what you need to be successful. We are up to date with ALL of our Textbooks. No Bait and switch. No hidden upsells. We invite you to compare......

WE HAVE THE LOWEST TEXT BOOK PRICES IN THE INDUSTRY!!!!!

1 Exam Prep takes pride in our students and in their success. We want you to pass your exam the first time, every time in the most cost efficient way. We offer the most comprehensive, easy to follow, easy to use exam preparation techniques in the industry. We offer both State and County Licensing Exam Prep Courses throughout the State of Florida. We have helped thousands of students successfully pass State and County Licensing Exams throughout Florida and we are seriously committed in helping you!

ALL OF OUR COURSES INCLUDE OUR PROVEN 4 POINT LEARNING SYSTEM UNRIVALED IN THE INDUSTRY
YOU WILL RECEIVE:

TABBING AND HIGHLIGHTING INSTRUCTIONS
The most comprehensive, up to date Tabbing and Highlighting instructions found anywhere in the industry. Our experienced instructors will provide you with more tabs, more highlights than any other exam prep school in the country. We know the material cover to cover. We show you what you need to know and where you will find it, when the pressure is on and the clock is moving.

TEST TAKING TECHNIQUES
Through a series of videos Rob Estell will guide you through proven and successful Test Taking Techniques he has shared with thousands of students. Learn the strategy on how to be the most efficient and effective on exam day. Learn how to manage the exam, the questions and the clock and make it work to your advantage

PRACTICE QUESTIONS AND ANSWERS
We provide our students with 1000's of Questions and Answers to help you prepare for your exam. We are continually updating and adding relevant questions with answers to prepare for the current exams. Our years of experience and thorough knowledge of the subject matter and testing formats allow us to provide you with the skills needed to address each and every question on the exam.

TEXTBOOK OVERVIEW
You will receive a high level summary on each textbook you receive and is required for your exam. The summary will outline the topics covered in the textbook, where these topics can be located in the textbook and the types of questions most likely to be answered in each textbook. You will also learn which parts of the textbook and which questions are aimed at a particular trade(s). Being thorough, efficient and confident is a huge advantage on exam day. Our Textbook Overview will help you manage your time and efficiency when the pressure is on and you need to stay focused.

OUR TEAM OF INSTRUCTORS HAVE THE EDUCATION AND THE EXPERIENCE AND ARE EXPERTS IN PREPARING YOU FOR PASSING YOUR EXAM. THEY HAVE OWNED THEIR OWN BUSINESSES, WORKED FOR DEVELOPERS AND BUILDERS, ENGINEERING FIRMS, UTILITY COMPANIES AND MUNICIPALITIES. THEY ARE DEDICATED TO YOUR SUCCESS AND WILL BE THERE WITH YOU EVERY STEP OF THE WAY. WE HAVE REGULARLY SCHEDULED CLASSES BUT WILL ALSO WORK WITH YOU ONE-ON-ONE; IN PERSON, VIA VIDEO CONFERENCING OR OVER THE PHONE. WHATEVER WORKS FOR YOU WORKS FOR US!

Other Services Offered
Application Assistance

Main Applications

⇒ Division I Application
⇒ Division II Application

Common Applications

⇒ Contractor Applications
⇒ Air A & B Applications
⇒ Plumbing Applications
⇒ Roofing Applications
⇒ Pool Applications
⇒ All Other Applications

Other Services

⇒ Corporate Registration
⇒ Credit Reports
⇒ DBA Registration
⇒ EIN Service

Book Packages & Tutoring Assistance

www.1examprep.com

1-877-804-3959

TABLE OF CONTENTS

TESTING INFORMATION & SCOPE OF EXAM — 6
TESTTAKING TECHNIQUES — 9
    Test Taking 101
    Time Management
PRACTICE EXAMS — 52
    Builders Guide to Accounting
        Accounting Methods
        Financial Statements
    AIA A201 – 701
    Contractor's Manual
        Circular E
        FLSA Questions
        Unemployment Compensation
        Lien Law
        Workers Compensation
        Rope, Wire and Chains
    Florida Statues: Chapter 455
    Florida Statues: Chapter 489
    Widget Examples
    Math
        Depreciation (No Salvage)
        Depreciation (With Salvage)
        Percentage of Completion Method
        Business Math
        Overtime
    Business and Finance Final Exams

Testing Information

The answers to the examination questions will be based on the editions listed below. Some of the test questions can be found on field experience and knowledge of trade practices. A different version of the books can be brought to the examination but **AT YOUR OWN RISK**. However, **ONLY ONE COPY** of each reference will be allowed into the test.

- **Photocopies will not be allowed unless the appropriate authorities (DBPR and the publishers) have given written authorization.**

- **Hand-written and typewritten notes are NOT allowed.**

- **Existing handwritten notes must be blackened out or whitened out completely, by the candidate, prohibiting legibility.**

- **Moveable tabs (e.g., Post-it® Flags) are NOT allowed.**

- **You will not be permitted to make any marks in your references during the examination.**

To speak to a Pearson Vue customer service representative about an exam reservation, please call **888-204-6230**

Approved References:

Builders Guide to Accounting

AIA A201 - 2017

AIA A401 - 2017

AIA A701 - 2018

2017 Contractors Manual

-Florida Statue Chapter 455, 2018 (it is a section from Contractor's Manual that is updated every year)

Examination Outline

The Business and Financial Management Examination is composed of:

One hundred twenty questions plus five pilot questions for a total of 125 questions

(Service Pool candidates will have **60 questions plus five pilot questions for a total of 65 questions**).

The test will be on a computer in the calm atmosphere of one of the testing centers at a time you have chosen.

You should be prepared to respond to examination questions on any of the content areas listed.

The percentage of questions shown for each content area may vary by as much as plus or minus three (3) percent.

Please, Rember **YOU** can bring these books with into the test:

Builders Guide to Accounting

AIA A201 - 2017

AIA A401 - 2017

AIA A701 - 2018

2017 Contractors Manual

Test Taking 101

Read each question carefully, and read all the answers before you make a selection. Once you choose the answer to a question, look it up in the reference books. This is especially important even if you believe you know the answer without looking it up. Examination questions are validated by state codes and reference books, not merely according to standard practice. By answering a question solely by experience, you could unknowingly give an incorrect answer. Although experience is helpful, it is still to your benefit to look up each answer.

Sample Question: The sky is _____.

    Blue

  Green

C. Red

    Orange

If the reference book says that the sky is green, guess what the correct answer to the question is the sky is green. If you mark blue, you are wrong for not following the directions of finding the correct answer in the book.

This is not a test of what you know, this is a text of problem-solving techniques. The State or County has research that has proven that all good business owners

MUST have problem-solving skills. If they do not possess these skills they have 4 times more of a chance of going out of business.

For best performance, go through the examination several times.

On the first pass, answer all the easy questions and write what book(s) (and chapter) you think the answer will be in.

On the second pass, take one book at a time and go from the front to the back of each book, by chapter, and answer the questions in the most efficient manner.

On each successive pass of the test, you will find the harder questions:

DO NOT SPEND 5 MINUTES ON A QUESTION UNTIL THE END OF THE TEST.

ALL MATH QUESTIONS ARE ATTEMPTED LAST.

DO NOT LEAVE ANY ANSWERS UNANSWERED. TAKE OU BEST GUESS, YOU WILL HAVE A 25% CHANCE OF GUESSING CORRECTLY. Many of my students have passed the test on this method only.

4. Relax, take a 30 second or 1 minute break every 30-45 mins.

5. You do not have to answer any of the very hard questions to pass the test. Learn to identify them early in the process, skip them and take 25% at the end.

Most people think that they have 2 minutes and 24 seconds per question(120 mins / 50 questions). Where actually if you do not attempt the very hard questions, you will have 3 mins and 10 seconds per question(120 minutes / questions).

Cross out the question on your test after you have found the correct answer.

This will ensure that you do not waste any time rereading a question that you have already answered, thus wasting your most valuable asset….. TIME!

Important Tip: If you are taking a paper and pencil exam, place a small check mark on the answer sheet next to any question you are going to skip.

This will do two things for you:

1. Reserve the answer line of the questions you are skipping

Instantly tell you which questions you need to look at again

Only one answer is right. If two answers mean the same thing, then they are both wrong. - Use scratch paper for math computations, and work neatly. Place the number of the question next to the computation, and draw a line to separate it from the rest of your work. That way, if you decide to go back and check your answers, you can easily find your math for a particular question.

Do not use your scratch paper as an answer sheet. Some candidates number down the side of the scratch paper, record their answers there and then transcribe them onto the answer sheet later. This practice is time-consuming and increases the risk of error. Even worse, some candidates do not remember to transcribe their answers and turn in blank answer sheets!

Remember: only the answer sheet will be scored.

• Your final score will be determined from the answers you record on the answer sheet. Allow time to record an answer for each question, but **DO NOT** mark more than one answer per question. After the time is called, no further marking of the answer sheet will be allowed. If you are unsure of an answer, it may be better to guess, since you will **NOT** receive credit for any question left blank. Select the closest or best answer for each question.

If you want to change an answer, make sure before you do so that you have clearly made an error and have seen the mistake. Then, erase carefully and completely.

When you have finished the examination, take a close look at your answer sheet. Check each line to make sure there is only one answer marked for each question and that you have completely erased any changes, check marks, or stray lines. Candidates taking computer-based tests may scroll back through the test to review and change answers if necessary.

After you finish the examination, raise your hand and wait for the examiner to check your papers for completeness before leaving your seat. You may then leave the room.

Filling Out Your Answer Sheet

For Paper and Pencil testing, you will be given a scan-able answer sheet and will be asked to bubble in your answers to each question. You may also be asked to bubble in some additional information such as your name, social security number, and the test number that is printed on your test booklet. You may be asked to sign a statement that you will comply with the test administration rules, procedures, and guidelines and that you will not divulge the test questions.

For computer-based testing, you will be using a keyboard and/or a mouse to enter your response to each question. You will be given time and a tutorial to familiarize yourself with using the keyboard or mouse to select your answers. If you complete your test and have time remaining, you will be able to review any or all questions and change your responses. You may also be asked to indicate agreement with a statement that you will comply with the test administration rules, procedures, and guidelines and that you will not divulge the test questions. (LOL)

STRATEGIES FOR TAKING A STATE OR COUNTY EXAM

The amount of time spent studying is not the only factor in being prepared. It is also very important to study efficiently. If you want to retain what you are studying you must set up a system. You are better off if you study for one hour in a quiet, private and relaxed atmosphere than if you study for 15 minutes at a time, 6 or 8 times a day. So start your exam preparation by setting up a schedule and picking an appropriate area.

Rules to help you study more effectively

Make sure that you know the meaning of words that are unfamiliar to you. Keep a list of the unknown words, look up their definitions and then keep going back to review the list.

Always try to follow your study schedule and plan.

Practice the rules for answering multiple choice questions while you are doing practice questions.

Find your weakest areas and then concentrate your study in those areas.

Write down problem questions and go back over them at a later date. Bring them to the class and ask the instructor to review questions.

Be sure to tab the books and become familiar with the tabs, indexes, and table of contents so you can find things quickly.

Time yourself, so you know how long you are spending on each question.

The Test Day

Remind yourself how well you will do on the exam.

Get a good night's rest. Get up early and remind yourself how well you will do on the exam. Eat a good breakfast. Remind yourself how well you will do on the exam.

Be sure to wear comfortable clothes. Wear or bring a sweater that you can add or remove depending on the room temperature. Remind yourself how well you will do on the exam.

Get to the exam site early. If you have to rush to find the site or get to the room you may not do as well on the exam. Remind yourself how well you will do on the exam.

Don't get nervous or excited. Remember, if all else fails, there is always another day.

General rules to answer multiple choice questions

1 Read the directions carefully and be sure that you understand them.

2 Look over the answer sheet and be sure you understand how to mark your answers.

3 Be carefully when transferring answers from the test to the answer sheet. Be sure to:

1 Mark answer completely,

2 Only mark one answer per question,

3 Make no extra marks on the answer sheet,

4 If you make an error, erase,

5 Be sure to mark the answer in the correct spot on the answer sheet. Repeat the answer to yourself as you transfer it to the answer sheet. And then check it again on the test sheet, repeating it.

1 Read the question carefully and be sure you understand what it is asking. Cross out any extraneous information. Read the question again.

2 Read all the answers before you make a choice. Quite often a "possible" answer is listed before the correct answer. **Don't be caught by this trap.**

3 Eliminate all choices that are wrong choices. After you read all the answers then cross out the wrong answers and chose from the remaining.

4 Never pick an answer because of a pattern to the answers on previous questions. There is no pattern. Just pick the answer you feel is correct.

5 Be aware of key words that may help select an answer. Absolute words, such as: always, never, only, all or none. These words usually indicate an incorrect answer. Limiting words such as: some, many, most, sometimes, usually, normally, occasionally, will often indicate the correct answer.

6 Skip over a question that gives you trouble or is taking too long to solve. Mark it in the question book so you can find it

later. Continue through the exam and come back to the question after you are completed. Be sure to save five minutes at the end of the test period, so that if there are any unanswered questions, you can at least guess at the answer.

10. Never leave a question unanswered. There is no penalty for a wrong answer.

11. Watch for negative question, such as, "Which of the following would make the statement false?"

12. How to make an educated guess. If there are four choices you have a 25% chance to pick the correct answer. But you may be able to improve those odds.

1. Eliminate the incorrect answers.

2. Look for answers with absolute or limiting words.

3. Look for answers with obviously the wrong sign (+ or -).

4. Look for two answers with the same meaning, they are probably both wrong.

5. Look for two answers with the opposite meaning, one of them may be correct.

1 If all else fails and you have to guess, always guess the same choice.

13. Be careful changing answers. Remember that your first guess is normally the best. If you have time at the end of the exam you should go back through the test. But, only change answers if you are sure that your first choice is incorrect, *ie.* you find a calculation error.

GOOD LUCK. Remember to keep reminding yourself that you will do fine and pass the exam!

If you have no confidence in yourself, you are twice defeated in the race of life. With confidence you have won before you've started-----MARCUS GARVEY

There are 24 hours in a day. If 8 of them are spent sleeping, that gives you 16 hours to get some efficient and productive study done, right?

It seems simple enough. There are plenty of hours in a day, so why is it so hard to use this time effectively, especially around exam time?

We've found that managing their time effectively is one of the things that students struggle the most with around exam time. However, time management is also one of the things that schools never teach – how frustrating?!

In the weeks leading up to study leave, every teacher you have for every class you go to seems to pile on the work: Mrs Gibb from English class tells you that you have to prepare 3 practice essays for both your visual and written texts, your Geography teacher Miss Wood expects you to do every past exam paper for the last three years before the exam, Mr West your Maths teacher says that you have to finish all of the questions in that darned AME textbook if you want to do well on the exam.

But they expect you to do all of this without giving you any time management tips. Mrs Gibb, Miss Wood and Mr West all fail to tell you how it's humanly possible to complete all of this work without collapsing when you walk into the exam hall.

That's where we come in!

Read on for the time management tips that your teachers never gave you!

1. Focus on what you have to study – not what you don't.
It seems obvious, but think of all the times you've sat down to study and you've ended up spending 2 hours studying the concepts you already know like the back of your hand.

It's easier to study the subjects you like. Studying the concepts that you're already confident in is a lot less challenging than studying the concepts that you find the most difficult, as your brain will have to work less to learn this information.

Studying what you already know is a bad time management strategy because you'll leave all the important stuff to the last minute meaning you won't have the time to cover these concepts in depth

The trouble with this tip is that it's often hard to decipher what you know and what you don't.

To figure out what you concepts you already know, and what concepts you still need to learn, complete a subject audit. A subject audit involves breaking down a particular subject into several points or sections and then analysing how well you know each of these points. You should spend most of your time studying those concepts that you have rated the most difficult. Find our study audit outline form here.

The key for effective time management is to review the easier material, but allow enough time to cover the harder concepts in depth so you're not left to study all of the most difficult concepts the night before the exam.

2. Work in sprints.
You may think that to have good time management skills you have to spend all of your time studying. However this is a misconception that many students hold.

Think of studying for exams like training for a marathon.

On your first day of training, you wouldn't go out and run 42kms. You would burn-out quickly due to a lack of prior training, and you would probably be put off running for a long time. This would not be a good way to manage your time. The better route to success would be to slowly work up to running the 42kms by running a bit further every day.

This simple idea of training in short bursts has been proven effective in all areas of human performance. You don't have to be a marathon runner to use this strategy!

When studying, you should start out small by studying in short, focused 'sprints' followed by brief breaks. Start by studying in 15 minute bursts followed by one 10 minute break. Over time, slowly increase the length of time you're studying (and breaking) for.

This strategy is effective because studying for short bursts promotes more intense focus, and will give your brain the time to process and consolidate information as opposed to studying for long periods of time which is not effective and may increase your chances of burnout.

Don't think of effective time management as studying for three hours straight with no breaks, think of effective time management as using your time wisely and in ways that will best promote retention of information.

Follow these steps to practice effective time management and become an expert studier (or marathon runner!) in no time:

1. **Set a timer for 15 minutes.**

2. **Put in some solid study until the timer goes off, making sure you're spending every minute working with no distractions.**

3. **Have a ten-minute break to check your phone, walk around, stretch, get outside etc.**

4. **Rinse and repeat.**

1   **Increase the amount of time you're studying for as you begin to feel more comfortable studying for extended lengths of time.**

1 Make a study system.

I'm sure you've been lectured by every teacher you've ever had to "make a study plan!!!" Study plans are effective for your time management, however they're sometimes hard to stick to.

Here at StudyTime, we find that the 'study system' is an effective strategy for really getting to the root of what you're studying. A study system is easier to stick to, and therefore fosters better time management skills, because it breaks tasks down into small chunks.

A study system is basically a simple list of steps that you can make to outline the steps you're going to take when you study. The list should start simple (4-5 things), but over time it should become more complex as you add steps to it.

Just like a workout plan at the gym or for sport, it will give you a clear direction of what action to take, making study much more efficient.

Over time, you can experiment with new study methods, and add them in to optimise the system.

Below is an example study formula that you could use when studying:

1   **Download the "Achievement Standard" from the NCEA website**

2   **Turn this into a checklist for what you already know and what you need to know**

3   **Break the checklist into main themes using a mind map**

4   **For each theme, make a summary sheet**

5   **After that, break down the key points of each summary and put these onto flash cards**

6   **Read through your notes and ensure you understand them, and then hit the flash cards**

7   **Test yourself on all of them first, then make two piles, one that's wrong and one that's right. Then redo the wrong pile again**

8   **Get someone else to test you**

9   **Practice exam papers – test yourself using exam papers from the past 2-3 years and time yourself**

10 **Work through the answers**

1. **Write a sheet of all tips/tricks i.e. things you got wrong in the practice exam papers**

2. **Redo exam paper and make model answers**

3. **Adjust flashcards if necessary i.e. make new ones based on the exam papers**

4. **Re-test all your flashcards**

Creating a study system will keep you on track and it will allow you to effectively plan out your time while studying.

4. Practice distributed learning.
Imagine your Maths teacher gave you seven equations to do for homework. How would you answer these questions? Would you do one question per day for seven days, or would you do all seven questions in one day?

You may think that it would be a better time management strategy to do all seven questions at once and get them over and done with. However, this is an ineffective way to manage your time.

The brain works better when it has time to process information. Neuroscience has shown that your brain needs time to consolidate information that has been newly learned, in order to form strong links between neurons and thus strong memories.

If the learning is done in one big chunk, you'll just forget it after three days. However, if you review it a day after, then you'll retain it for seven days.

When making a study schedule, you should space out when you study for each subject. For example, don't spend one day studying English, then the next day studying Maths, then the next day studying Biology. Instead, you should alternate studying for these subjects throughout the day. Do one hour of Maths, then one hour of English study, then one hour of Biology, and so on.

This is a much better way to manage your time, because the more often you review a concept, the more solidified it will be in your mind. This is because there will be more time to consolidate this into your memory. Also, taking breaks between reviewing certain concepts will give your brain time to process the information.

Try it out!

Florida Department of
Business & Professional Regulation

Division of Professions
Bureau of Education & Testing
Candidate Services Examinations
1940 North Monroe Street
Tallahassee, Florida 32399-0791
Phone: 850.488.5952 • Fax: 850.487.9757

Ken Lawson, Secretary   Rick Scott, Governor

Business & Finance Computer Based Examination (CBT) Reference List
Valid October 2014 – January 2016 Revised

Candidate Name: _____ Date: _____

Candidate Number: _____

The answers to the examination questions will be based on the editions listed below. Some of the questions will also be based on field experience and knowledge of trade practices. Editions earlier or later than those listed below can be brought to the examination but AT YOUR OWN RISK. However, only one copy of each reference will be allowed into the examination.

Photocopies will not be allowed unless the appropriate authorities (DBPR and the publishers) have given written authorization. Hand-written and typewritten notes are NOT allowed. Existing hand-written notes must be blackened out or whitened out completely, by the candidate, prohibiting legibility. Moveable tabs (e.g., Post-it® Flags) are NOT allowed. You will not be permitted to make any marks in your references during the examination.

CHECK THE CILB EXAM LATEST FLYER UPDATE, IF APPLICABLE AT:
http://www.myfloridalicense.com/dbpr/servop/testing/ConstructionReferencePage.html

Any materials other than those approved will be stored along the wall of the exam room. The Department is **NOT** liable for loss of or damage to candidates' property. Candidates are advised to clearly label all belongings.

ONLY BRING THESE BOOKS IN FOR BUSINESS & FINANCE:

Ref #	Titles
R1	***Florida Statutes Chapter 455, 2013***, Division of legislative Information Services, Rm 704 Claude Pepper Building, 111 West Madison St, Tallahassee, FL 32399-1400, 800-342-1827. http://www.flsenate.gov/Laws/Statutes/2012/Chapter455

AIA documents are listed below.
The American Institute of Architects, PO Box 60, Williston, VT 05495. or Florida Association of AIA, 104 East Jefferson St., Tallahassee, FL 32301.
http://www.aiafla.org/Store_Contract-Documents.cfm

Ref #	Document #	Titles
R5	A201	***General Conditions of the Contract for Construction***, 2007.
R6	A401	***Standard Form of Agreement between Contractor-Subcontractor,*** 2007.
R7	A701	***Instructions to Bidders***, 1997.

LICENSE EFFICIENTLY. REGULATE FAIRLY.
WWW.MYFLORIDALICENSE.COM

R37	**Builder's Guide to Accounting**, Michael C. Thomsett, Copyright 2001. Craftsman Book Company, 6058 Corte del Cedro, Carlsbad, CA 92009. www.craftsman-book.com/
R50	**Contractors Manual**, 2013 (which includes the 2012 Circular E). Association of Builders and Contractors Institute, Inc., 3730 Coconut Creek Parkway, Coconut Creek, FL 33066. (Ph 866.930.4222)

CONTRACTORS
BUSINESS & FINANCIAL MANAGEMENT
EXAMINATION CONTENT INFORMATION

Revised October 2009

The Business and Financial Management Examination is composed of 120 questions (Service Pool candidates will have 60 questions). It will be administered in one session via computer in the calm atmosphere of one of our convenient testing centers at a time of your choosing.

You should be prepared to respond to examination questions on any of the content areas listed. Questions asked and content areas tested on previous examinations should not be assumed to be the only possible questions to be asked or content areas to be tested on this examination.

The percentage of questions shown for each content area may vary by as much as plus or minus three (3) percent. Please refer to the Candidate Information Brochure and the Reference List for additional information.

Content Area A   11%
Establishing the Contracting Business

Determining the Business Organizational Structure
knowledge of business structure laws and regulations
knowledge of fiduciary responsibilities of officers and directors
knowledge of open vs. closed corporations
knowledge of organizational charts and chain of responsibilities
knowledge of state and local licensure requirements
knowledge of tax advantages and/or liabilities for various business structures

Develop the Business Plan
knowledge of accounting practices
knowledge of local marketplace
knowledge of scope of contractor license

Establish Relationships with Other Professionals
knowledge of accountant specialization
knowledge of attorney specialization
knowledge of insurance types and limitations
knowledge of underwriting requirements for bonding

Acquire Fixed Assets
knowledge advantages/disadvantages of business location
knowledge of advantages/disadvantages of lease vs. purchase

Obtain Insurance
knowledge of accounting practices
knowledge of advantages/disadvantages of various types of insurance
knowledge of coverages and limitations of insurance

Content Area B   26%
Managing Administrative Duties

Develop the Business
knowledge of availability of staffing for business operation
knowledge of income sources knowledge of markets and market share

Determine Outsourced Services

Determine Business Overhead
knowledge of FICA
knowledge of advertising costs (business cards, dues, printing, etc.)
knowledge of communication costs (cell phones, land lines, etc.)
knowledge of cost of sales (travel expenses)
knowledge of federal unemployment (FUTA)
knowledge of general liability rates knowledge of lease expenses
knowledge of loan financing expenses (interest, etc.)
knowledge of Medicare rates
knowledge of rent costs
knowledge of state unemployment (SUTA)
knowledge of utility costs
knowledge of worker's compensation

Preparing Bids/Proposals
knowledge of accounting principles
knowledge of AIA documents

knowledge of business projections/goals current status
knowledge of company overhead
knowledge of contract documents
knowledge of contract law
knowledge of cost of financing projects
knowledge of costs associated with growth
knowledge of general conditions costs of projects
knowledge of how to review contracts knowledge of how to write offer
knowledge of insurances associated with labor rates
knowledge of labor productivity knowledge of statute of frauds
knowledge of taxes associated with labor rates knowledge of components of valid contract

Purchase Materials/Supplies
knowledge of depreciative costs
knowledge of fundamentals of Uniform Commercial Code
knowledge of inventory system operation (FIFO, etc.)
knowledge of invoice approval systems knowledge of negotiating skills knowledge of purchasing systems knowledge of receiving systems knowledge of state sales tax laws knowledge of statute of frauds knowledge of vendors in area

Prepare Invoices/Draw Requests knowledge of basic math skills
knowledge of calculation of percentage of work completed
knowledge of contract/subcontract documents knowledge of how to prepare invoices/draw requests
knowledge of lien laws

Develop a Safety Program
knowledge of drug testing regulations knowledge of MSDS sheets knowledge of OSHA regulations

Maintain Insurance
knowledge of general terms and definitions used in policies
knowledge of insurance policies
knowledge of limits of insurance
knowledge of various types of insurance knowledge of various types of risk

Managing Contracts knowledge of contract law knowledge of contract scope
knowledge of job completion schedules
knowledge of lien laws

knowledge of mediation and arbitration processes
knowledge of local building code requirements
knowledge of tort law
knowledge of risk management

Content Area C   10%
Managing Trade Operations

Schedule Trade Operations knowledge of critical path method (CPM) knowledge of delivery times knowledge of manufacturing times knowledge of requests for information (RFI) knowledge of sequencing trades knowledge of submittals/approval/fabrication process

Maintain OSHA/Safety Records
knowledge of document/record retainage requirements
knowledge penalties for non-compliance with OSHA

Purchase/Order Materials & Supplies
knowledge of accounting skills knowledge of basic math skills knowledge of job schedules knowledge of negotiation skills knowledge of organizational skills
knowledge of plan reading skills knowledge of quality control knowledge of quantity take-offs knowledge of terms and abbreviations on invoices

knowledge of types of building materials

Leasing/Purchasing Equipment knowledge of cost of operation of equipment knowledge of depreciation
knowledge of equipment operation knowledge of forecasted use of purchased equipment
knowledge of interest costs for financing
knowledge of maintenance knowledge of salvage resale values

knowledge of support equipment required for equipment
knowledge of tax credits associated with purchases
knowledge of training needs for equipment
knowledge of transportation costs for equipment

Manage Material/Tool/Equipment Inventory knowledge of equipment maintenance procedures
knowledge of inventory methods

Content Area D   32%
Conducting Accounting Functions

Manage Accounts Receivable
knowledge of accounting principles
knowledge of basic math skills
knowledge of computer skills
knowledge of lien laws

Manage Accounts Payable
knowledge of accounting principles
knowledge of basic math skills
knowledge of computer skills
knowledge of how to calculate discounts
knowledge of lien laws

Manage Cash Flow
knowledge of accounting
knowledge of banking
knowledge of basic math skills
knowledge of financial ratios

File Tax Forms & Returns knowledge of accounting principles
knowledge of basic math
knowledge of federal tax laws
knowledge of property tax laws
knowledge of record keeping requirements
knowledge of sales tax laws
knowledge of state tax laws

Track Job Costs
knowledge of accounting principles
knowledge of basic math

Calculate Employee Payroll
knowledge of accounting
knowledge of state & federal tax laws
knowledge of basic math
knowledge of employment laws
knowledge of employment/labor laws

knowledge of hierarchy of garnishments

Content Area E   6%
Managing Human Resources

Hire New Employees knowledge of employment laws
knowledge of discrimination laws
knowledge of interviewing skills
knowledge of required forms for new hires
knowledge of background checks

Develop Human Resource Policies & Procedures
knowledge of employment/labor laws
knowledge of OSHA
knowledge of chain of custody (drug tests)
knowledge of insurance regulations

Evaluate Employees
knowledge of employment/labor laws

Content Area F   15%
Complying with Government Regulations

Comply with Federal Laws & Regulations
knowledge of FEMA (immigration components)
knowledge of OSHA
knowledge of tax laws
knowledge of National Pollution Discharge Elimination System (NPDES)
knowledge of environmental laws

Comply with State Laws & Regulations
knowledge of Chapter 455 F.S. (Business & Professional Regulation)
knowledge of Chapter 713 F.S. (Liens)
knowledge of 61G4 F.A.C.
knowledge of Worker's Compensation Laws/DOR Sales/Use Tax
knowledge of Chapter 489, Part 1 F.S (Construction Contracting)
knowledge of required continuing education
knowledge of CEU credit records
knowledge of license holder responsibilities

Division of Professions Bureau of Education and Testing Examination Development Unit 2601 Blair Stone Road Tallahassee, FL 32399-0791 Phone: 850.487.1395 Fax: 850.922.6552

Candidate Information Booklet for the Construction Licensure Examinations (Excluding Plumbing)

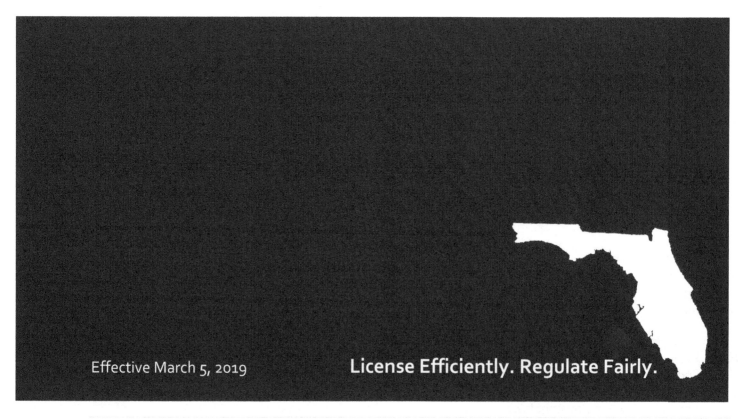

Effective March 5, 2019

License Efficiently. Regulate Fairly.

Table of Contents

Introduction 2
   Testing Locations and Reservations 2
   Making your Test Reservations 2
   Telephone or Internet Reservations 2

The Examination 3
   Examinations at a Glance 3
   References 4
   Pilot Testing 4
   Test Taking Advice 5
   Supplies 5
   What to Bring 5
   What not to Bring 6

Administrative Policies 6
   Change and Cancellation Policies 6
   Absence Policy 7
   Admission to the Examination 7
   Admission Procedures 7
   Late Arrivals 8
   Rules for the Examination 8
   Apparel 8
   Change of Address 8
   Change or Correction of Name 9
   Special Testing Accommodations 9

Scoring Information and Grade Notification 9
   Scoring Procedures 9
   Notification of Results 9
   Examination Review and Fees 9
   Review Session 10
   Challenge Process 10
   Reexamination Information 10

Appendix 11
   Points of Contact 11
   Address Change Form 12
   Common Abbreviations and Definitions 13

Statement of Nondiscriminatory Policy
The Department of Business and Professional Regulation does not discriminate among candidates on the basis of age, sex, race, religion, national origin, handicap, or marital status.

Please save this document for future reference.
Visit our website at:
http://www.myfloridalicense.com/DBPR/examination-information/

Introduction

The Department of Business and Professional Regulation has contracted with Professional Testing, Inc., to register candidates, develop, and score professional examinations for the Construction Industry Licensing Board. Individuals desiring to sit for construction examinations are required to apply directly with Professional Testing, Inc.

To apply online: http://www.floridaexam.com/
To apply by phone: 407.264.0562

All construction examinations, except Plumbing Contractor, are administered in computer-based testing format. After a candidate has been approved by Professional Testing, Inc., they may schedule to sit for their examination(s) by contacting the department's examination vendor, Pearson VUE.

The Department of Business and Professional Regulation has retained the services of Pearson VUE to schedule, administer, score and report the results for computer based testing (CBT). Pearson VUE is a provider of assessment services and provides testing and support services to regulatory agencies, national associations, state agencies, and private industries.

Your examination(s) will be administered on computer. The CBT system eliminates the use of paper, pencil and answer sheets. Before you begin the examination, you will have an opportunity to go through a tutorial on the computer. The computer is very simple to operate; it should only take you a few minutes to learn how to use it.

The screen features a variety of function buttons to help candidates navigate through the examination. The function buttons are located in the same position throughout the test. Candidates can mark a question for review, move forward or backward one question at a time, or move to a specific question. The summary screen, which can be accessed at any time during the examination, shows candidates the following:

0. Number of questions answered
1. Number of questions unanswered and/or skipped
2. Time remaining for the examination

Testing Locations and Reservations

To locate a Pearson VUE Test Center near you, as well as to check that site's availability, use this link to view the vendor website for more details: https://home.pearsonvue.com/fl/construction.

Making your Test Reservations

Candidates that already know their candidate identification number are reminded that they do not have to wait for a "Confirmation"/ "Authorization" letter to make their reservation.

Telephone or Internet Reservations

Call 1.888.204.6230 and a Pearson VUE Customer Care Associate will help you to select a convenient examination date and location and answer any questions you may have. The best

2

times to call for a reservation are: Monday – Friday (8am – 11pm), Saturday (8am – 5pm), and Sunday (10am – 4pm). You may register as far in advance as you would like to test based on seat availability. However, it is strongly recommended you call at least five (5) business days before the examination date desired since reservations are made on a first-come, first-served basis.

Candidates may register via the Internet. You may submit a request via the Internet to Pearson VUE website at https://home.pearsonvue.com/ twenty-four (24) hours a day, seven (7) days a week, provided you include a credit card number, electronic check or voucher, and valid email address. A reservation confirmation will be returned to you via email. Examination reservations may be canceled or changed via the Internet.

Please have the following information when you call to make an examination reservation:

- Your authorization notice
- Candidate Identification number listed on your authorization notice
- Your full name, address and a daytime telephone number
- The location of the test center you desire
- The name of the examination you will be taking
- Credit card number, check, or voucher

The Examination

The Department of Business and Professional Regulation issues various construction licenses. Visit the Construction Industry Licensing Board website to find out more about the categories: http://www.myfloridalicense.com/DBPR/construction-industry/.

This Candidate Information Booklet (CIB) provides general information common to all of the examinations. Specific information describing the content areas tested and references materials for each examination can be found in the "Examination Content Information" and "Reference List" documents for each trade. In addition to the specific content areas listed for each examination, knowledge of basic mathematics is required for each part of the examination. All questions will be multiple-choice with four (4) alternative answers and will be equally weighted.

It is your responsibility to obtain the Examination Content Information and Reference List for the examination you are scheduling. You can contact the Department or refer to our web site for the most current information. Visit this link on the web for current examination information: http://www.myfloridalicense.com/DBPR/examination-information/construction-examinations/.

Candidates must pass all required examinations to be licensed. The examinations you take will depend upon which license you are seeking and whether you already hold another construction license. Passing candidates applying for examination in an additional category may be exempt from retaking the Business and Financial Management portion of the examination.

Examinations at a Glance

This chart provides you with information about each of the construction industry examinations. In order to obtain a license you must pass all of the required examinations for your specialty. Division I contractors (General, Building, and Residential) must pass three examinations: Business & Finance, Contract Administration, and Project Management. Division II contractors (all other specialties) must pass two examinations: Business and Finance and General Trade Knowledge.

Examination	# of Scored Questions	Time (hours)	Administration
Business & Finance	120	6.5	Daily CBT
Business & Finance Service Pool	60	3.5	Daily CBT
Air Conditioning "A"	130	7.5	Daily CBT
Air Conditioning "B"	80	5	Daily CBT
Mechanical Contractor	130	7.5	Daily CBT
Glass and Glazing	80	5	Daily CBT
Marine Specialty	80	5	Daily CBT
Irrigation	80	5	Daily CBT
Pollutant Storage	80	5	Daily CBT
Pool – Commercial	80	5	Daily CBT
Pool – Residential	80	5	Daily CBT
Pool – Service	60	5	Daily CBT
Gas Line	80	5	Daily CBT
Gypsum Drywall	80	5	Daily CBT
Roofing	80	5	Daily CBT
Sheet Metal	80	5	Daily CBT
Solar	80	5	Daily CBT
Specialty Structure	80	5	Daily CBT
Underground Utility	80	5	Daily CBT
GC – Contract Administration	60	4.5	Daily CBT
GC – Project Management	60	4.5	Daily CBT
BC – Contract Administration	50	4.5	Daily CBT
BC – Project Management	50	4.5	Daily CBT
RC – Contract Administration	45	4.5	Daily CBT
RC – Project Management	45	4.5	Daily CBT

For the Plumbing Candidate Information Booklet, please visit:
http://www.myfloridalicense.com/DBPR/examination-information/candidate-information-booklets

References

Visit the link below to find an up to date reference list:
http://www.myfloridalicense.com/DBPR/examination-information/construction-examinations-reference-lists/

Pilot Testing

The Examination may contain a small number of experimental or "pilot test" questions. The purpose of including pilot test questions within the examination is to expand and improve the bank of questions from which future examinations will be drawn. This is a common practice used by many national and state examination programs and is a critical step in ensuring the continued reliability and validity of these examinations.

In the event that pilot test questions are included within the examination, these questions will NOT be counted when computing scores. Additional time will be given for answering the pilot test questions. The time allowed for testing has been evaluated to ensure there is adequate time for completing test questions and pilot questions.

Pilot questions are NOT identified. If the pilot questions were identified, many of the candidates would skip them, and the results would not be valid. The development of a good examination requires accurate candidate response information for the pilot questions.

Test Taking Advice

The advice offered here is presented primarily to help you demonstrate knowledge and maximize your chances of passing the examination.

> Read all instructions carefully.
> For best results, pace yourself by periodically checking your progress. This will allow you to make any necessary adjustments.
> Be sure to record an answer for each question, even the items about which you are not completely sure. You can note the questions you wish to reconsider on the computer testing system and return to them later.
> Alert a Proctor or Test Center Manager to any problems that may occur during the examination. Do not wait until the examination is over to inform someone about a problem.

Supplies

It is expressly understood by each candidate that the State of Florida, and/or the Department of Business and Professional Regulation, and the Department's staff hereby assume absolutely no liability of any nature whatsoever for any items of the candidate's personal property which may have been brought to, left at, or left outside the examination site.

It is further understood that the candidate's admission to the examination shall hereby constitute the candidate's full, knowing, and complete waiver of any and all such claims against the State of Florida, and/or the Department of Business and Professional Regulation, and the Department's staff.

What to Bring

All candidates will be required to bring the following items to the testing center on the day of the examination:

> Personal items are not permitted in the examination room. Any personal items such as toiletries, snacks, etc. must be encased in a clear plastic bag, no larger than 8" X 11" in size and kept in the locker provided by the vendor.
> Two forms of valid signature identification, one of which is government issued: driver's license, state identification card, passport or military identification card.
> **Student or employment I.D. cards and photo bearing credit cards are not acceptable as picture bearing identification.** Candidates will not be admitted

5

without showing proper identification. Your name and address must match what was submitted on your application.

Calculators are permitted if they are silent, hand-held, battery-operated, nonprinting, and without an alphabetic keypad. Solar calculators are not recommended.

To better serve our "English as a second language" candidates, the Bureau of Education and Testing is permitting the use of foreign language translation dictionaries during the examination. Translation dictionaries shall contain word-for-word or phrase translations ONLY. Dictionaries that contain definitions of words, explanations of words, or handwritten notes may NOT be used.

Electronic translation dictionaries are NOT recommended as most will have more than word-for-word or phrase translations, an alphabetic keypad, have mathematical formulas and stored memory capabilities. Should these electronic translation devices have these capabilities; these devices WILL be rejected by the Proctor or Test Center Manager in NOT being suitable for the test site environment.

Testing Center staff will inspect and approve each dictionary before it can be used during the examination. In order to maintain security and to ensure fairness to all candidates, candidates are limited to the use of a single dictionary.

If you have any questions concerning acceptable translation dictionaries, please contact the Bureau of Education and Testing at 850.487.1395.

What not to Bring

Unauthorized supplies, those not listed in this Candidate Information Booklet, will be subject to removal by the Department's representative at the examination site.

The following items are NOT allowed in the examination room:

- Cameras, tape recorders, or computers
- Pagers, electronic transmitting devices, or telephones (watches with alarms or beepers should be set so that they will NOT sound or go off during the examination administration)
- Any bound or loose leaf reference materials and notes
- Dictionary, thesaurus, or other spelling aids
- Canisters of mace, pepper spray, or other personal defense items
- Purses, briefcases, portfolios, fanny packs, or backpacks

Administrative Policies

Change and Cancellation Policies

If you wish to cancel your exam, you must contact Pearson VUE **2 days** prior to your scheduled appointment. Cancelling an exam less than **2 days** prior to your appointment or missing your exam may result in forfeiting your exam fees.

Absence Policy

If you are unable to attend the examination for which you were scheduled, you may be excused for the following reasons:

- Your illness or that of an immediate family member
- Death in the immediate family
- Disabling traffic accident
- Court appearance or jury duty
- Military duty

All candidates seeking excused absences must submit written verification and supporting documentation of the situation to Pearson VUE no later than four days after the original examination date. Documentation of medical absences must have the original signature of the medical practitioner. Stamped signatures will NOT be accepted. **You will be required to pay your examination in full, and possibly reapply to DBPR, if you do not show up for your exam appointment.**

Admission to the Examination

When registering at the test center, you will be required to have the following items:

Two forms of valid signature identification, one of which is government issued: driver's license, state identification card, passport or military identification card.
Student or employment I.D. cards and photo bearing credit cards are not acceptable as picture bearing identification. Candidates will not be admitted without showing proper identification. Your name and address must match what was submitted on your application.

Admission Procedures

Please report to the test center thirty (30) minutes prior to your scheduled examination. As part of the checking–in process, a photo will be taken of the candidate prior to taking the exam. This photo will be visible on the candidate's exam result report. The Test Center Manager will assign you a seat and assist you with the computer. You may take up to fifteen (15) minutes to complete the tutorial and the Test Center Manager will answer any questions you may have about the computer testing unit at this time.

The time you spend on the tutorial will NOT reduce the time allotted for taking your examination. When you feel comfortable with the computer testing unit, you may begin your examination. The time of the examination begins the moment you look at the first question on your examination.

Your specific reporting time will be given to you when you make your examination reservation. Please allow yourself sufficient time to find the test center. Make sure you have all necessary documentation before you report for registration.

At the completion of the examination, your score report will provide instructions on the next step of the licensure process.

Late Arrivals

Test Center Managers will review the daily schedule for that day to determine if the candidate can be accommodated due to tardiness. If the tardiness was caused by an emergency (i.e., car trouble, traffic accident, etc.) the candidate must provide documentation of the event. If the candidate cannot be accommodated due to unexcused tardiness, they will be liable for the test fee for that day in addition to the new test fee and classified as a "No Show."

Rules for the Examination

The examination materials, documents, or memoranda of any kind are not to be taken from the examination room.

Listen carefully to the instructions given by the Test Center Manager and read all directions thoroughly. Test Center Managers are NOT qualified or authorized to answer questions concerning examination content. However, if you have any procedural questions, they will do their best to assist you.

If you have a concern about the content of an examination question, please request a "Candidate Comment Form."

You must have the Test Center Manager's permission to leave the examination room. You will NOT be allowed additional time to make up for time lost.

Smoking will not be permitted in an examination room or in the restrooms, based on the October 1985 Florida Clean Indoor Air Act.

Do not bring food into an examination room. If applicable, a lunch break will be provided. Drinks are allowed in spill proof containers. Children and visitors are NOT allowed in the test center.

You are NOT permitted to take personal belongings such as briefcases, large bags, study materials, extra books, or papers into the testing room. Any such materials brought into the testing room will be collected and returned to you when you have completed the test. Pearson VUE and the Department are NOT responsible for lost or misplaced items.

Under NO circumstances will you be permitted to work beyond the time allotted for the examination. Time limits are generous; you should have ample time to answer all questions and check all work.

Apparel

Please dress comfortably, but appropriately, for the examination. The examination room is usually climate controlled. However, it is not always possible to maintain a temperature suitable to each candidate, and from time to time there are maintenance problems beyond the Department's or Pearson VUE's control. It is suggested that you bring a sweater or jacket in case the temperature is cooler than your individual preference.

Change of Address

If an address change occurs after your examination administration, please make corrections at http://www.myfloridalicense.com/DBPR/construction-industry/construction-industry-renew-and-manage-my-license/ or by completing the change of address form provided at the end of this booklet.

Change or Correction of Name

If you have a name change or correction, please send a copy of notarized legal documentation Professional testing, Inc. immediately.

Special Testing Accommodations

The Department of Business and Professional Regulation certifies that it will comply with the provisions of the Americans with Disabilities Act (42 USCG Section 12101, et seq.) and Title VII of the Civil Rights Act, as amended (42 U.S.C.2000e, et seq.), in accommodating candidates who, because of a disability, need special arrangements to enable them to take an examination.

All applicants for an examination or a reexamination who desire special testing accommodations due to a disability must submit an application to the Special Testing Coordinator prior to each exam. The application can be found at:
http://www.myfloridalicense.com/dbpr/servop/testing/documents/ada_applic.pdf.

The application for accommodation must be completed and returned to the Bureau of Education and Testing at:

Department of Business and Professional Regulation
Bureau of Education and Testing
Special Testing Coordinator
2601 Blair Stone Road
Tallahassee, Florida 32399-0791

For more information regarding special testing accommodations, please our visit webpage at:
http://www.myfloridalicense.com/DBPR/examination-information/special-testing-accommodations/.

Scoring Information and Grade Notification

Scoring Procedures

All questions are equally weighted. Examination scores are reported as percentage scores. The minimum percentage score needed to pass has been set at seventy percent (70%). Scores on the construction exams are <u>NOT</u> rounded to the nearest percent.

Notification of Results

All candidates will receive an official photo-bearing exam result report immediately following completion of their examination. Please verify that all information is correct on your exam result report prior to leaving the test center.

Examination Review and Fees

Candidates who fail an examination are entitled to review the questions they answered incorrectly, under such terms and conditions as may be prescribed by the Department of Business and Professional Regulation. Candidates are entitled to review only their most recent examination. The candidate shall be permitted to review only those questions the candidate answered incorrectly.

The request to review must be made within 21 days from the date of the examination and can be scheduled by going online to: https://home.pearsonvue.com/ or by calling 1.888.204.6230. The same security requirements observed at the examination will be followed during the review session. Reviews will be held at a Pearson VUE testing center.

The fees associated with reviewing a Computer Based Testing examination are included in the following link:
http://www.myfloridalicense.com/dbpr/servop/testing/documents/cbt_exam_admin_Fee_2016.pdf.

Review Session

The review session is considered to be an extension of the examination administration. Only the candidate may attend the review session. Proper identification is required to obtain entry. There will be no talking or note taking of any kind. Candidates are usually given one-half of the exam administration time. For example, a 2 hour and 30 minute examination will only receive 1 hour and 15 minutes to review. Candidate will not be able to see their original exam book since it is not retained, after the exam.

Challenge Process

Written challenges are accepted for DBPR developed examinations. Candidates are given an opportunity during the review session to note in writing, on the computer, any objections they have to questions answered incorrectly. The challenges are forwarded to the Bureau of Education and Testing for review by a Psychometrician and subject matter experts to determine if there is any merit to the candidate's objection.

The response time to challenges, on average, is approximately 21 days. Due to the confidential nature of the examinations, the only response you will receive is "credit" or "no credit" for each challenged question. Credit will only apply to the candidate who reviewed and challenged. Per Rule 61-11.017(g) the candidate's challenges must be submitted in writing during the scheduled review. Any challenges or supporting documentation submitted after the candidate has left the review room shall not be accepted.

For informal review and formal hearing procedures visit:
http://www.myfloridalicense.com/DBPR/examination-information/examination-reviews-and-hearings/.

Reexamination Information

Before you are allowed to sit for the examination again you are required to reapply directly with Professional Testing, Inc.

To reapply online: http://www.floridaexam.com
To reapply by phone: 407.264.0562

10

Appendix

Points of Contact

Please contact the appropriate office for questions regarding the following:

Examination Scheduling, Grade Notification and Change of Address
Professional Testing, Inc.
P.O. Box 691226
Orlando, Florida 32869
Tel: 407.264.0562
Fax: 407.264.2977

Requests for Special Testing Accommodations Department of Business and Professional Regulation Bureau of Education and Testing Special Testing Coordinator
2601 Blair Stone Road
Tallahassee, Florida 32399-0791
850.487.1395
BETSpecialTesting@myfloridalicense.com

Examination Review
Pearson VUE, Inc.
Customer Care at 1.888.204.6230
Website: https://home.pearsonvue.com/
Fax-Back System at 1.800.274.8920

Formal Hearings
Department of Business and Professional Regulation
Bureau of Education and Testing
2601 Blair Stone Road
Tallahassee, Florida 32399-0791
850.487.1395

Licensure Application and Fees
Department of Business and Professional Regulation
2601 Blair Stone Road
Tallahassee, Florida 32399-0791
850.487.1395

Visit our website at:
http://www.myfloridalicense.com/DBPR/examination-information/

11

Please fill out the change of address form below and return to:

Professional Testing, Inc.
P.O. Box 691226
Orlando, Florida 32801
Tel: 407.264.0562 Fax: 407.264.2977

Address Change Form

Please type or print in the appropriate spaces below if you have a change of address correction.

Name: _____

*Social Security #: _____

Examination Date: _____

Candidate Number: _____

Phone Numbers: _____
                      Area Code/Home Number   Area Code/Work Number

Old Address: _____

New Address: _____

Signature: _____

*Under the Federal Privacy Act, disclosure of Social Security Numbers is voluntary, unless specifically required by Federal Statutes. In this instance, Social Security Numbers are mandatory pursuant to Title 42, United States Code, Sections 653 and 654; and Sections 455.203(9), 409.2577, and 409.2598, Florida Statutes. Social Security Numbers are used to allow efficient screening of applicants and licensees by a Title IV-D child support agency to assure compliance with child support obligations. Social Security Numbers must also be recorded on all professional and occupational license applications, and will be used for licensee identification pursuant to the Personal Responsibility and Work Opportunity Reconciliation Act of 1996 (Welfare Reform Act), 104 Pub.L. 193, Sec. 317.

Common Abbreviations and Definitions

Abbreviations	Definitions
DBPR	Department of Business and Professional Regulation
F.S.	Florida Statute
F.A.C.	Florida Administrative Code
BET	Bureau of Education & Testing
ADA	Americans with Disability Act
CBT	Computer Based Testing
CE	Continuing Education
CIB	Candidate Information Booklet
BCAIB	Building Code Administrators and Inspectors Board
ICC	International Code Council
FBC	Florida Building Commission
CILB	Construction Industry Licensing Board
ECLB	Electrical Contractors' Licensing Board
FAQ	Frequently Asked Questions

Division of Professions
Bureau of Education & Testing
Candidate Services Examinations
2601 Blair Stone Road
Tallahassee, Florida 32399-0791
Phone: 850.488.5952 • Fax: 850.487.9757

Jonathan Zachem, Secretary

Rick Scott, Governor

Frequently Asked Questions Examination Scheduling and Fees Construction Industry Licensing Board (CILB)

1. **Q.** When did the CILB Business and Finance examination part go computer based testing?

   The CILB Business and Finance examination began CBT scheduling and administration on January 5, 2009.

   Q. How do I apply to take the CBT Business and Finance Examination?

   Contact or apply to Professional Testing Inc. (PTI) by either calling 407-264-0562 or online at: http://www.floridaexam.com/.

   Q. What are the fees to register for the Construction examination?

   ### Scheduling:

   ### All parts of the examination:

   Credit card payment of $215.00 to PTI is now available. *(Covers the examination development, application and administration fees). If paying by check, submit $135.00 payable to PTI and a separate $80.00 check to PTI made payable to DBPR.
   An $80.00 examination administration fee is payable to Pearson VUE, the CBT contracted vendor, at the time of scheduling for the Business and Finance examination.

Updated June 26, 2012

Contract Administration, Project Management, or Trade Knowledge only:

Fee of $135.00 examination development and application fee to PTI, $80.00 examination administration to DBPR. Credit card payment of $215.00 to PTI is acceptable.

Business and Finance Exam only:

A $135.00 examination development and application processing fee payable to PTI and an $80.00 examination administration fee payable to Pearson VUE, the CBT vendor, at the time of scheduling the examination.

Q. I have registered with PTI for the entire examination but I haven't been scheduled with Pearson VUE.

After registering with PTI, allow 5 to 7 days for DBPR to update and send your authorization to Pearson VUE.

Q. How do I pay Pearson VUE for the Business and Finance?

Candidates must pay the examination administration fee at the time of reservation by credit card or electronic check, personal checks are not accepted. Candidates who cannot use these payment options should contact Pearson VUE to arrange to pre-pay the examination fee. **Payment are not accepted at the test center.** Examination fees are non-refundable and non-transferable.

Q. Can I pay the $80.00 DBPR examination administration fee via Credit or Debit card?

Yes, DBPR examination administration fee must be paid to PTI at the time of Applying and credit cards are accepted. You can pay PTI $215.00 by credit card.

Q. When will I get my authorization to schedule the Business and Finance Examination?

Authorizations with scheduling instructions will be mailed or emailed to each candidate from Pearson VUE after the application and/or retake application has been approved. Once you receive your authorization, contact Pearson VUE toll free, 888-204-6230 to schedule your CBT Business and Finance examination or online at http://www.pearsonvue.com/.

Q. What will I need to schedule my CBT examination?

You will need your authorization, social security number, form of payment, and know the name of the examination you've been authorized to take. Also view the following instructions on this web link: http://www.myfloridalicense.com/dbpr/servop/testing/documents/prof_reg_faq.pdf

Q. Will I be allowed to take my reference books inside the examination room and will there be ample space for storage?

Yes.

Q. How much time is allotted for the Business and Finance CBT examination?

You will have 6 hours and 30 minutes to complete your examination. Pool Service category candidates will receive 3 hours and 30 minutes to complete the examination. This includes pilot items.

Q. Will I receive a grade report at the exam site?

Yes. Once you have completed your examination.

Q. Why do scores have fractional values?

Since we are dividing the number of correct answers by the total number of questions on the exam to calculate a percentage, it is possible to get scores with fractional values when the number of questions on the examination is not a multiple of 100. For example, the Business and Finance examination consists of 120 questions. A candidate who answered 88 questions correctly would get a score of 73.33% (88 divided by 120.) For all examinations where the number of "real" questions is a multiple of 10, 70% correct will correspond to a whole number, for example 84 divided by 120 is exactly 70%.

Q Why aren't scores rounded up?

A The CILB rules prohibit rounding of scores. A candidate must achieve <u>at least</u> 70% in order to pass the examination. Rounding would not make any difference since the minimum passing score for almost all of the examinations comes out to be a whole number, the only exceptions to this are the Residential Contractor Contract Administration and Project Management examinations, which have 45 questions each. 70% of 45 equals 31.5; however, it is impossible to answer only half a question correctly. A candidate who answered 31 out of 45 questions correctly would have a score 68.89% which if rounded to the nearest whole number would be 69%, neither of which is a passing score. Candidates must answer 32 out of 45 questions correctly to pass these examinations.

The Plumbing General Trade Knowledge examination has a total of 160 possible points. To pass this examination a candidate must have a score of 112 out of 160 possible points. A score of 111 out of 160 comes to 69.38% which would be rounded down to the nearest whole number, not up because the decimal is less than .50.

Q How are Isometrics Drawings scored?

A The Isometric drawings are graded by teams of three licensed plumbing contractors who serve as examiners (Subject Matter Experts). Teams of examiners will score the Isometric drawings. Each examiner independently scores every drawing as pass or fail on eight different criteria (legibility, orientation, flow, angles, piping, labeling, vents, and fixtures.) At least two out of the three examiners must agree that the criteria have been met in order for points to be awarded. The points awarded for all correct criteria are added together and converted to a 10 point scale to determine the score for each drawing. The number of points awarded for each drawing is then added to the total number of correct answers obtained on the multiple choice questions during the morning and afternoon sessions. This figure is then divided by the total number of possible points (160) to obtain the percentage correct score.

Q Do I have to do the Plumbing Isometrics?

A The 5 Isometric Drawings on the Plumbing examination are worth 10 points each, for a total of 50 points. There are 110 multiple choice questions that are worth 1 point each. Thus a total of 160 points is the maximum possible score. 50 out of 160 points equals 31.25%. Since the minimum passing score is 70%, it is not possible to pass this examination unless at least some points are earned for the Isometrics.

Q. If I fail the CBT Business and Finance examination, how do I re-apply?

You must submit a retake examination application to PTI and pay the appropriate examination development and application fee of $135.00, and the examination administration fee of $80.00 to Pearson VUE when you reschedule.

17. **Q.** If I fail one or more portions of the examination, do I have to retake all parts?

No. Rule 61G4-16.009, Florida Administrative Code, states, "A candidate shall be required to retake only the tests on which he or she failed to achieve a passing score or failed to appear to take when scheduled." Starting November 1, 2011, a candidate must pass all parts of the examination within four years of the first administration attempt.

Q. How soon may I retake the examination if I fail the Business and Finance portion?

You must wait 21 days before you re-take the examination again.

Q. Will I be allowed to review my Business and Finance examination if I fail?

Yes, however only your last administered failed examination. You must request the Review within 21 days from the Grade Report date. You will schedule your review with Pearson VUE as you would the examination. The review fee is $35.00 payable to Pearson VUE,

Q. When I pass all parts of the CILB examination, how do I apply for my license?

To apply for your license with DBPR, please visit the Department website at: http://www.myfloridalicense.com/dbpr. Include with your license application, the appropriate fees as mentioned in the application fees below:

FEES:
IF ALL EXAM PARTS WERE PASSED PRIOR TO JANUARY 1, 2009:
Applying for initial licensure from **MAY 1st** of an **EVEN YEAR** through **AUGUST 31st** of an **ODD YEAR** – $409

OR

Applying for initial licensure from **SEPTEMBER 1st** of an **ODD YEAR** through **APRIL 30th** of an **EVEN YEAR** – $309

IF ANY EXAM PART WAS PASSED AFTER JANUARY 1, 2009: Applying for initial licensure from **MAY 1st** of an **EVEN YEAR** through **AUGUST 31st** of an **ODD YEAR** – $249

OR

Applying for initial licensure from **SEPTEMBER 1ST** OF an **ODD YEAR** through **APRIL 30th** of an **EVEN YEAR** - $149

If you have additional questions, please feel free to contact the DBPR Customer Contact Center at 850.487.1395 or Bureau of Education and Testing (BET) at 850.488.5952

Updated June 26, 2012

1 Exam Prep
Builder's Guide to Accounting
Questions and Answers

All the following are normally required for a loan application except a _____.

    an income statement
    a balance sheet
    a tax return
    retained earnings

The only reasonable way to assign overhead is in proportion to what?

    income
    total expenses
    cost of materials
    direct labor hours

All the following can be accomplished as the result of a good cash budget except:

    plans for the use of excess funds when they are available
    reconciliation of the bank statement
    preparation for tax liabilities
    cash availability for day to day operations

When According to the Builder's Guide to Accounting, when estimating job costs, all the following should be included except for _____.

    labor
    material losses
    fixed overhead
    construction materials

What can a contractor determine at the break even-point?

    various yields for different types of jobs
    the kind of work that is needed to reach a volume goal
    growth potential
    the least amount of sales needed to break even, assuming costs and expenses remain reasonably constant

A contractor computes the percentage of gross profit to sales volume over a number of months. The contractor finds that gross profit is decreasing in relationship to sales. Of the factors listed below, which is the most likely explanation?

    not enough volume of work
    sales prices are to high
    lack of control over costs
    material thefts are decreasing

A contractor will complete a project in 2 years. At the end of the first year, annual gross receipts were $8,500,000. What is the amount that the gross receipts for the second year cannot equal or exceed in order to use the completed contract method of accounting?

    $5,000,000
    $6,500,000
    $10,000,000
    $11,500,000

Which accounting method is the most acceptable for recording income and expenses for large jobs which last longer than one tax year?

    percentage of completion
    completed contract
    combined accounting
    cash accounting

Billings that have been mailed out by a firm, but for which payment has not been made, are called____

    unearned income
    receivable
    deferred income
    accounts payable

When determining a bid for a job, which is considered a fixed overhead expense?

    Code office staff
    materials needed for the job
    purchases of small tools
    rental of equipment to be used only for that job

A valuable method of preparing a cash budget for builders who have wide variations in business volume from month-to-month month is the:

    cash movement method
    percentage of completion method
    capitalized cost method
    source and application of funds method

What prepared document would contain current information about revenue that is due to a company?

    cash flow statement
    bank balance statement
    aging of accounts receivable
    income statement

If the current ratio is too low, it may be raised by _____.

    converting cash to fixed assets
    retaining profits within the business to buy fixed assets
    replacing short-term borrowing with long-term borrowing
    increasing its operating costs

According to Builder's Guide to Accounting, the break-even point _____.

    distinguishes between the various yields of the different jobs and job types
    can help the contractor decide what kinds of work he or she needs to reach a volume goal
    encourages growth
    indicates the minimum sales you need to break even

Which one of the following is an incentive to pay an invoice early or when due?

    credit
    rebate
    discount
    additional contracts

Which is the best method to check an estimate in order to eliminate as many errors as possible?

    have another estimator take the original estimate and recheck the figures and computations
    compare the original estimate with an estimate from a similar project
    perform the estimating process a second time and compare it with the initial estimate
    have another estimator make an independent estimate and compare it to the original estimate

All the following statements about bad debts are correct except _____.

    the contractor should make every effort to try to collect bad debt before writing them off as a loss
    the reserve for bad debts reduces working capital
    the older an outstanding balance becomes, the more likely it is to become a bad debt
    bad debt losses have little or no effect on cash budgeting

When a construction company is applying for a loan, most banks require all the following items except?

    a current balance sheet
    a current income statement
    last year's federal income tax return
    last year's state income tax return

Which is NOT true concerning a good cash budget?

- assists in planning operations for seasonal business
- encourages over or under buying of materials
- helps in obtaining credit
- prepares for tax liabilities

Freight charges on material shipped to a job by the supplier are defined as what type of cost?

- direct
- incidental
- indirect
- overhead

For payroll record keeping it is suggested to _____.

- have duplicate time cards properly signed and dated
- list payroll checks in separate check registers
- give separate stubs only to employees paid overtime that pay period
- give your accountant the names and amounts of each check given to each employee

To convince a lender to extend a loan, a contractor must demonstrate that he or she:

- will not be under undue financial strain from the loan payments
- has the loan amount in an account
- has a proven track record for performing excellent work
- has a minimum current ratio of 3 to 1

Which of the following is considered a type of accrual?

- cash or other payments received
- billings mailed out, but not yet paid
- anticipated profit from uncompleted work
- estimated cost of work not yet completed

Which would be considered an intangible asset?

- cash
- patents
- fixed assets
- prepaid assets

Which is not characteristic of a trial balance?

- it serves as a means of checking whether the general ledger is in balance
- it facilitates the preparation of the financial statement
- it shows at a glance the distribution of the individual accounts
- it shows the current trend in the accounts receivable

When sales equal the total of fixed, sales expenses and direct costs, this is referred to as _____.

- cash flow
- available cash
- balance sheet
- breakeven point

Real turnover is an example of what kind of ratio?

- combined
- current
- income
- expense

Deferred income should be entered on a balance sheet as _____.

- current liability
- long term liability
- deferred credit
- current asset

What is the purpose of preparing an income statement?

- to borrow construction funds or secure personal credit
- B to divide information into various categories to prepare the cash flow statement
- C. to show control of costs and expenses, the volume of business, and income yield
- D. to predict profits over a period of time

Which is a method of improving cash flow?

- maintaining a high inventory
- taking advantage of discounts
- converting all cash sales to accounts receivable
- paying off liabilities

Who is eligible for Small Business Association loans?

    all building contractors in the Unites States
    only company presidents
    applicants who cannot obtain a loan from local banks
    applicants who are recommended by a local bank

When a piece of equipment is sold, why is it necessary to book the transaction separate from regular sales?

    treated as a variable expense
    receives different tax treatment
    transaction is not taxable
    gains or losses must be used to adjust gross profits

Which of the following is an example of an accrual entry?

    depreciation and amortization entries
    entries to record payroll taxes
    entries to record automatic loan payments
    entries to record purchase of material stored at jobsite

To establish an hourly cost for a piece of equipment, the contractor needs to consider all the following except _____.

    estimated life of the equipment
    cost of the equipment, less salvage value
    replacement cost of the equipment
    estimated average hours of use

Which of the following best describes the accrual method of accounting?

    transactions are recorded when cash is received or paid
    no receivables or payables are recorded on the balance sheet
    revenues are recognized when earned, even though no cash has been received
    payables are recorded before receivables are received

Which of the following is not a depreciation method recognized by Builder's Guide to Accounting?

    declining balance depreciation
    accumulated cost depreciation
    sum of the years' digits depreciation
    straight line depreciation

A typical purchase order should include all of the following *except* _____.

    the billing and delivery address
    a preprinted purchase order number
    sales tax for purchase and for resale
    an authorized signature

What financial information summarizes the existing conditions of a business?

    the balance sheet
    the cash flow statement
    the income statement
    the statement of retained earnings

The term "lapping" refers to _____ taken from the business by moving outstanding balances from one customer account to another.

    cash
    equity
    liabilities
    receivables

What ratios compare accounts on the balance sheet to accounts on the income statement?

    quick assets
    combined
    income
    current

What type of cost basis inventory valuation method uses the current market value of material as it is used?

    specific cost
    first in-first out
    last in-first out
    cost-plus inflation

Which is not used when calculating goods sold to average inventory ratio?

    labor
    materials purchased
    all other direct costs
    total monthly averages

All the following are effects of inventory control *except* _____.

    reducing the need for storage space
    quickly providing needed material
    increasing exposure of materials to possible theft or arson
    minimizing investment of capital in inventory

A contractor would use the completed contract method of accounting when _____.

    most of the jobs last longer 24 months
    the contractor wants a more realistic picture of actual financial performance
    most of the jobs are small, or one-time work jobs with single installment payments
    the contractor has annual sales in excess of $10,000,000

Controlling purchases using a purchase order system could help you control _____.

    accounts receivable
    bad debts
    job costs before you are committed
    payroll

What is an advantage of a bad debt reserve?

    it reduces tax liability for earned profit
    it increases assets
    it increases profits
    it simplifies accounting procedures

Who is eligible for Small Business Administration (SBA) loan programs?

    all construction businesses located in the United States
    corporations operated on a non-profit basis
    businesses with fewer than 100 employees regardless of sales volume
    construction businesses with annual sales volume of $17 million and less than 100 Employees

What can a contractor determine at the break-even point?

    various yields for different types of jobs
    the kind of work that is needed to reach a volume goal
    growth potential
    the least amount of sales needed to break even, assuming costs and expenses remain reasonably constant

A contractor with serious cash flow problems, but with high volume of work _____.

    should first try to improve cash flow through budgeting
    should first try to increase the volume of work
    should first try to lower the volume of work
    would likely qualify for a loan

An equity account is best described as the _____.

    original value of the business
    original inventory of the business
    original investment of the owners
    total value of loans from the bank

Regarding the inventory value, individual labeling is done for what cost basis method?

    first in first out
    last in first out
    perpetual inventory
    specific cost

When a contractor writes off the expense of a piece of equipment over time, that process is called_____

    accelerated depreciation
    depreciating a fixed asset
    depreciation of intangible property
    depreciating a current asset

The volume of business that must be maintained in order to avoid a loss is the _____.

    percentage of sales
    net worth
    available cash
    breakeven point

Which inventory cost-basis valuation method assumes that the first materials purchased are the first used?

    specific cost
    first in first out
    first in last out
    last in first out

All the following are generally found on an invoice except _____.

    a description of materials
    the sales price of the materials
    the terms of the invoice
    the balance of the customer's account

Current liabilities include the portion of long term debt for equipment purchases that is payable within _____.

    30 days
    90 days
    180 days
    365 days

What does gross sales less direct costs equal?

    gross profit
    net profit
    income from operations
    net sales

What is the sum of assets minus liabilities?

    net profit
    net worth
    gross sales
    gross profit

All the following would be considered variable overhead expenses except _____.

    payroll taxes on office salaries
    field office trailer rental
    worker's compensation insurance
    bad debts

Successful builders control their costs *best* at which time?

    at the end of each week
    during each phase of the work
    immediately prior to approving invoices
    in bi-weekly meetings with the owner present

An indicator of how well a company can meet its current obligations is the company's _____.

    expense ratio
    debt to capitalization ratio
    current ratio
    income to net worth ratio

During the year, a firm used several independent contractors to perform various services. Each of these services involved payments in excess of $600 to the independent contractor performing the services. The independent contractors were not employees of the company. What is the company's responsibility for reporting the earnings of these contractors to the Internal Revenue Service (I.R.S.)?

    the company must immediately file a Form W-4 for these independent contractors
    the company must file Form 1099-MISC to report total payments of $600 or more to these contractors
    the company must carry the contractors as employees and report their earnings along with the company's hourly or salaried personal
    the company has no responsibility. The independent contractors are responsible for reporting their earnings to the I.R.S.

When preparing financial statements, accruals are used to record _____.

    lump sum payments
    income earned but not yet received
    cash transactions
    prepayments on a future contract

Which jobs would not require use of the straight percentage of completion method?

    jobs longer than two years in duration
    firms that require periodic, progressive recognition of profit from their jobs
    construction jobs producing revenue greater than $10 million
    jobs costing $1,000 - $5,000 which take approximately one week to complete

One of the most practical and useful cash controls available is _____.

    a daily cash summary
    a quarterly cash summary
    a secure petty cash box
    keeping petty cash receipts

All the following are procedures included in the budget process except _____.

    analyzing the results
    consulting with your accountant
    preparing the budget
    taking action to control expenses

When figuring overhead, which is a fixed expense?

- small tools
- operating supplies
- equipment rental
- advertising

The best way to control equipment costs is good_____.

- maintenance
- scheduling
- financing
- reports

In order to establish an hourly cost for a bulldozer for job allocations, which of the following would *not* apply?

- cost of equipment less salvage value
- operating costs involving gas, oil, and accessories
- repairing and maintenance costs
- unpredictable job site conditions

When preparing a financial statement for a lender before applying for a loan, it is best to first_____.

A. accumulate current assets to improve the cash position
B. reduce current liabilities
C. try to decrease the current ratio
D. try to increase the volume of business

All current liabilities include equipment that is payable within _____.

- 30 days
- 90 days
- 180 days
- 365 days

Which item below is not a fixed asset?

　　　Office furniture $ 1,243
　　　Land $35,000
Trucks $ 6,410
Inventory $20,000

　　　inventory
　　　land
　　　office furniture
　　　trucks

When using the inventory ratio method, a high ratio indicates _____.

　　　average inventory
　　　high inventory
　　　high market average
　　　low inventory

The first step in preparing a financial statement at the end of an accounting period is to put together _____.

　　　a supplementary schedule
　　　a trial balance
　　　an income statement
　　　the closing adjustments

A definite plan for fixed assets should include all of the following *except* _____.

　　　records of maintenance cost
　　　a determination if proposed equipment is useful for the job
　　　a policy establishing depreciation rates
　　　a study of lease vs. purchase options

All the following are advantages of leasing except _____.

　　　an immediate tax deduction is available for the cost of monthly leases
　　　the equipment will receive regular use
　　　no large investment or financing commitment is required
　　　it allows the contractor the chance to evaluate equipment before buying it

Which one of the following assets is eligible for depreciation?

　　　land
　　　warehouse
　　　inventory
　　　intangible property

Good inventory control _____.

    increases exposure to theft
    maximizes the need for storage space
    maximizes investment in capital inventory expenditures
    reduces taxes and insurance costs

Which one of the following is a variable overhead expense?

    utilities
    postage
    labor payroll taxes
    rent

When the plotted job progress curve does not swing up soon enough, the contractor _____.

    will make a higher overall job profit
    will finish early
    needs to delay scheduled labor and material
    has over-estimated the cost

Which statement regarding leases is not true?

    a lease-purchase agreement for equipment may require little or no initial investment
    depreciation can be claimed on equipment that is lease-purchased
    an immediate tax deduction is not available for the cost of monthly leases
    for equipment that will be used for a brief period of time, leasing is cheaper than owning

A complete cash budgeting plan _____.

    does not address loan payments
    ignores tax liabilities
    controls the purchase of materials
    addresses the type of business of business organization used

A schedule of equipment time should include all of the following *except* _____.

    scheduled time
    the job number
    consideration for adverse weather
    repair time

Which of the following is a current asset?

    accounts payable
    accounts receivable
    construction equipment
    furniture

When determining a project bid, which of the following expenses is considered an overhead expense?

    costs of recruiting laborers for that job
    materials needed for that job
    purchases of small tools
    rental of equipment to be used only for that job

1 Exam Prep – Builder's Guide to Accounting - 2   15

1 Exam Prep
Builder's Guide to Accounting
Questions and Answers

DPage 317
DPage 228
BPage 173, 174
BPage 227
DPage 178, 179
CPage 272
CPage 25
APage 25, 26 & 32

    Page 25, completed contract method is used for small jobs. Answer B is eliminated.

    Page 26, combined accounting method is not recommended for long duration contracts and can complicate record keeping. Answer C is eliminated.

    Page 32, cash accounting method deals with cash entries only (cash changing hands) and is does not reflect a company's true financial condition. Answer D is eliminated.

BPages 43 – 46
APage 142 and 143
APage 176
CPage 46
CPage 174, 175
DPage 179
CPage 59
BPage 11 or 225
DPage 63 – 67
DPage 317
BPage 173, 174
APage 115
BPage 126
APage 316
BPage 11 or 237
BPage 253
DPage 250 and 252
DPage 179
APage 273

28. C   Page 191
29. C   Page 249
30. B   Page 262
    CPage 318, 319
    BPage 170
    DPage 237
    CPage 159, 160
    CPage 11 or 237
    BPage 163
    > Note: there is no such thing as accumulated cost depreciation Sum-of-the-years depreciation is one of the methods still being used under the old rules

    CPage 116, 117 Note: Key word - "not for resale")
    APage 247
    APage 181
    BPage 270
    CPage 120
    DPage 121
    CPage 121, 122
    CPage 25
    CPage 116
    APage 64
    DPage 318
    DPage 179
    APage 174
    CPage 253
    DPage 120
    BPage 252 (only fixed assets are depreciated)
    DPage 179
    BPage 120
    DPage 44 and Figure 3-6
    DPage 155
    APage 248
    BPage 247
    APage 142, 143
    > Payroll taxes on office salaries is a fixed expense

60. B   Page 189
61. C   Page 269
62. B   Page 138
    BPage 106, 107

Under the accrual method of accounting, revenue is considered earned when services are rendered and expenses are considered to be incurred when services are received.

64. D   Page 25
65. A   Page 180
66. B   Page 144
67. D   Page 142
68. B   Page 228
69. D   Page 159,160
70. B   Page 174
71. D   Page 253

APage 252 or 327 (Long-Term Assets)
Fixed assets are also referred to as long-term assets.

73. D   Page 121
74. B   Page 250
75. B   Page 156
76. B   Page 169
77. B   Page 162
78. D   Page 121
79. C   Page 142
80. C   Page 308

CPage 169, 170
CPage 173, 174
CPage 159
BPage 327 or 252
CPage 142, 143

Answer C is the correct answer because the purchases of small tools is an indirect expense (variable expense) not related to any particular job but part of an overhead expense.

Answer A is wrong because costs of recruiting laborers for that job is a direct cost

Answer B is wrong because materials needed for that job is a direct cost

Answer D is wrong because rental of equipment to be used only for that job is a direct cost

1 Exam Prep
Builders Guide to Accounting
Accounting Methods

Booking income is the process of:
    Making the journal entry in the books.
    Showing the income as income in the books.
    Writing down the amount of the check on your bank deposit slip.
    Transferring the income entry from the cash journal to the general ledger.

Under the percentage-of-completion method, income is booked:
    Only as it is received.
    Only when it is due and payable.
    Only as a percentage of the total bid, based on the percentage the job is completed as of that date.
    Only when the project is completed.

When percentage-of-completion income has been booked, any amounts received over that are:
    Returned to the payee as an overpayment.
    Kept on hand until they can be booked, preferably in a secured, locked area.
    Deposited and recorded as unearned income.
    Kept as additional, unrecorded profit.

When percentage-of-completion income is higher than the amount received, the underpayment is:
    Recorded as accrued income.
    Written off as a loss.
    Written off against miscellaneous expense.
    An unrecorded net loss.

Under the completed-contract method, income is booked:
    According to the schedule of payments agreed to at the time the contract starts.
    As cash payments are made.
    At the end of the job.
    When inspections of each completed phase have been completed and signed off.

The problem with completed-contract accounting is:
    The books don't necessarily reflect an accurate picture of how you're doing.
    All the income and profit shows up in the same year, even when some of it occurs over two or more years.
    The bookkeeping might require special records to keep track of receivables and payables.
    All of the above.

Earned income accounts are:
    Asset accounts.
    Liability accounts, even though they aren't really liabilities, but deferred income.
    Profit and loss accounts.
    None of the above.

Under the percentage-of-completion method, deferred income accounts are:
- Asset accounts.
- Liability accounts, even though they aren't really liabilities, but deferred income.
- Profit and loss accounts.
- None of the above

When earned income and deferred income entries are made in your books:
- The entries are netted against each other.
- Only the larger of the two entries is allowed under current rules.
- The differences are billed to customers before the tenth of the following month.
- Reversal entries are entered in the books for the previous month's earned and deferred totals.

Percentage-of-completion and completed-contract method are both variations of:
- Double-entry bookkeeping.
- Accrual accounting.
- Cash accounting.
- Single-entry accounting.

The cash method of accounting requires that entries be made:
- When source documents are received.
- When transactions are known and final.
- When cash changes hands.
- When bills get sent out.

In accrual accounting, payments that are received but not yet earned are:
- All profit.
- Returned to the customer.
- Accrued.
- Unearned.

The estimated total cost of a job is $822,000. Total costs paid to date are $295,900. The percentage-of-completion on this job is _____.
- 2.7%
- 27%
- 3.6%
- 36%

When a part of each progress billing is held back, it's called:
- Accrual.
- Retainage.
- Deferred income.
- Backup withholding.

The purpose of percentage-of-completion accounting is to:
- Allow multiple jobs to be worked on at the same time.
- Report income only as jobs are completed.
- Report income progressively when periods exceed one tax year.
- Simplify the bookkeeping and accounting task.

1 Exam Prep
Builders Guide to Accounting – Accounting Methods

1. b. pg. 34
2. c. pg. 23-24, 28
3. c. pg. 23-24
4. a. pg. 24
5. c. pg. 25
6. d. pg. 25-26
7. a. pg. 27
8. b. pg. 32
9. d. pg. 31, 35
10. b. pg. 26
11. c. pg. 32
12. d. pg. 23-24
13. d. pg. 23-24 math: $295,900 ÷ $822,000 = .3599 (or 36%)
14. b. pg. 24
15. c. pg. 24

1 Exam Prep
Builders Guide to Accounting
Financial Statements

The Balance Sheet:
    Summarizes income, costs, and expenses, and shows the balance between income and profits.
    Summarizes cash flow for the period covered.
    Shows the status of assets, liabilities and net worth as of a specific date.
    Includes assets, liabilities, net worth, cash flow, and profit or loss, all on one page.

The Income Statement:
    Is prepared only if there is a net profit for the year; when there is a loss, a loss statement is prepared instead.
    Summarizes income, costs, and expenses for a specified period of time.
    Is vastly different than the profit and loss statement.
    Is always prepared on the accrual basis.

The Statement of Cash Flows:
    Is a summary of cash received and cash paid during the year.
    Is simply an income statement, prepared on the cash basis.
    Is a relatively obscure financial statement that is of little real value.
    All of the above.

The reserve for bad debts is:
    An asset
    A reduction of current assets
    Represents amounts expected to become collectible within one year
    An amount that has nothing to do with taxes

The basic formula for the Balance Sheet is:
    Assets plus liabilities equals net worth.
    Liabilities less net worth equals assets.
    Assets plus net worth equals liabilities.
    Assets less liabilities equals net worth.

The trial balance is:
    A worksheet prepared to determine whether net profit is high enough.
    A test of the general ledger's balance.
    An exercise used primarily in first-year bookkeeping classes.
    A worksheet used only when preparing a budget.

Supplementary schedules:
    Should be used to give your financial statements a professional look.
    Are used only by accounting firms when they prepare audited statements.
    Should be used whenever you need to explain something in greater detail than you show on the primary statements.
    Are used only for legal disclosures.

A contingent liability is:
- A potential debt that might or might not become an actual liability.
- A liability that's used only for the purposes of developing a conservative statement.
- A liability that isn't due for one year or more.
- Deferred income and really not a liability at all.

Retained earnings are:
- The accumulated earnings left in the company from one year to the next.
- Earnings kept by the owner and not reinvested.
- Real earnings for tax purposes.
- Another name for capital stock.

The tax provision is:
- Inclusive only of Federal taxes.
- A way of letting the reader of the financial statement view profitability without considering taxes
- An actual bank account, containing a reserve for all estimated unpaid taxes.
- d. An important planning account category for partnerships

The purpose of the Statement of Cash Flows is to:
- Provide a summary of budget variances for the year.
- Show where likely sources for borrowing money can be found.
- Summarize changes in working capital and other Balance Sheet accounts during the year.
- Prove that the numbers on the Income Statement add up.

Footnotes are an important part of the financial statement because:
- Some financial information isn't reported on the statements.
- Some liabilities might or might not come to be.
- One-time items have to be reported to explain big changes for the year.
- All of the above.

A "contingent" liability is one that:
- May be paid at a later date if you desire.
- Is reported as a footnote to the Balance Sheet.
- Is properly classified as a bad debt.
- None of the above.

Closing adjustments are intended to:
- Make your financial statement accurate by allowing for last-minute changes.
- Reduce tax liabilities when possible by reclassifying expenses.
- Force a balance when you find errors in your books.
- Maximize non-cash expenses in the current year.

Working capital refers to:
- The balance in your bank account.
- All of your current assets.
- The net difference between accounts receivable and accounts payable.
- The net difference between current assets and current liabilities.

1 Exam Prep
Answers - Builders Guide to Accounting - Financial Statements

1. c. pg. 17
2. b. pg. 17 and 248
3. a. pg.18
4. b. pg. 68, 69
5. d. pg. 17
6. b. pg. 250
7. c. pg. 252
8. a. pg. 253
9. a. pg. 254
10. b. pg. 255
11. c. pg. 18
12. d. pg. 256
13. b. pg. 256
14. a. pg. 251
15. d. pg. 256

1 Exam Prep

Builders Guide to Accounting Questions

Part 1

1) A contractor's bids a job using the followings costs and cost factors:

Subcontractors:	$37,500.00
Labor Costs:	$ 6,700.00
Materials:	$ 9,200.00
Sales Tax on Materials Only:	6.00%
Job Overhead:	42.00% of labor costs only
Mark-up:	8.00%
Bond:	0.75%

Based on the figures above, the total bid is _____ . Assume no other costs or cost factors other than those given above.

A. $56,766.00
B. $60,104.00
C. $61,307.00
D. $61,767.00

2) Given: A General Contractor's summary of estimate for a construction project is as follows:

General Conditions and Office Overhead		$ 15,000.00
Job Conditions and Job Overhead		$ 32,000.00
Construction Plan, Tools & Equipment		$ 15,000.00
Subcontracts Total Bid		$ 450,000.00
Subcontracts Performance Bond Rate Markup		0.75%
Labor Estimate		$ 300,000.00
Labor Taxes and Insurance Rate Markup		33.00%
Materials Estimate		$ 850,000.00
Materials Sales Tax Rate Markup		6.00%
Profit Markup		10.00%
First $100,000	$9.50 per	$ 1,000.00
Next $100,000	$9.25 per	$ 1,000.00
Over $500,000	$8.50 per	$ 1,000.00

If all costs to be considered are included in the figures above, the total bid in the project is:

A. Between $2,004,000.00 and $2,008,000.00
B. Between $2,008,000.00 and $2,012,000.00
C. Between $2,012,000.00 and $2,016,000.00
D. Between $2,016,000.00 and $2,020,000.00

BALANCE SHEET AS OF DECEMBER 31

ASSETS		LIABILITIES	
Cash:	157,024.00	Accounts Payable:	311,407.00
Total Accounts Receivable:	302,627.00	Total Current Liabilities:	44,107.00
Total Current Assets:	580,983.00	Total Long Term Debt:	47,109.00
Property and Equipment	54,122.00		
Total Assets:	**$643,171.00**	**Total Liabilities:**	**$402,623.00**

3) Refer to the provided financial information. The company's working capital as of December 31st is?

$178,360.00
$322,467.00
$536,876.00
$640,548.00

Refer to the above financial information. During the month of January, the net effect of all business operations was:

Cash decreased:	$ 42,437.00
Accounts Receivable increased:	$ 32,116.00
Current Liabilities and long term Debt Decreased:	$ 2,474.00

The net worth of the company at the end of January was _____?

$168,469.00
$232,701.00
$240,548.00
$250,869.00

A construction company is considering borrowing money to purchase a new piece of heavy equipment that will replace an existing piece of equipment. The old equipment and the new equipment will both be rented at an average of 25 hours per week to customers who will be charged $45.50 per hour of use. During the last year the old equipment averaged $2,000.00 per month for all repair and maintenance costs.

The new equipment repair and maintenance cost is estimated at $1,200.00 for the year. The average amount that will be borrowed during the first year of operation (average principal due) will be $75,000.000.

The new equipment will depreciate $12,000.000 in value during the first year. Considering only the repair and maintenance costs on the old and new equipment, the interest cost on the loan for the new equipment and the value depreciation of the new equipment, what is the least simple interest rate on a loan that will allow the same gross profit during the first year of operation of the new equipment as the last year operation of the old equipment?

A. Less than 13.5%
B. Between 13.5% and 14.0%
C. Between 14.0% and 14.5%
D. Greater than 14.5%

The earned income, figured on the percent completed method, for a construction company for the year ending December 31st was $2,474,086.00. The general and administrative expenses for this period were $127,532.00. The cost of goods sold (contract costs) for this period was $2,314.098.00. For single family residential construction performed earned income was 55% of the total, general and administrative costs were 60% of the total, and contract costs were 50% of the total.

The net earnings (loss) from single family residential construction for the year was:

A. Profit of $203,698.00
B. Profit of $127,239.00
C. Loss of $76,459.00
D. Loss of $159,988.00

BAD DEBT STUDY:

Period	Actual Bad Debt Losses	Total Credit Sales	Month End Accounts Receivable (not including retainage)
January	$ 700.00	$ 18,800.00	$ 21,200.00
February	$ 0	$ 15,400.00	$ 19,300.00
March	$ 510.00	$ 22,500.00	$ 26,400.00
April	$ 430.00	$ 27,600.00	$ 32,400.00
May	$ 0	$ 22,400.00	$ 28,600.00
June	$ 840.00	$ 19,700.00	$ 22,400.00
July	$ 750.00	$ 26,600.00	$ 33,100.00
August	$ 0	$ 24,400.00	$ 30,700.00
September	$ 0	$ 19,400.00	$ 25,300.00
October	$ 650.00	$ 18,100.00	$ 20,900.00
November	$ 0	$ 23,200.00	$ 28,500.00
December	$ 0	$ 26,400.00	$ 31,300.00

Refer to the Bad Debt Study above. The current entry to reserve for bad debts for the month of April should be:

A. Less than $660.00
B. Between $660.00 and $680.00
C. Between $681.00 and $700.00
D. More than $700.00

8) Refer to the Bad Debt Study above. What is the year-to-date bad debt ratio at the end of September?

0
1 to 27
1 to 54
1 to 61

9) A contractor was involved in three distinct types of work during the last 12 months:

Type A work: Had a total volume of sales of $450,000.00 with a net profit of $27,000.00
Type B work: Had a total volume of sales of $860,000.00 with a net profit of $30,100.00
Type C work: Had a total volume of sales of $180,000.00 with a net profit of $25,200.00

A. Less than 5.200/0
B. Between 5.205% and 5.40%
C. Between 5.41% and 5.60%
D. More than 5.60%

A contractor has established a $50,000.00 line of credit. During the first six months the average amount borrowed was $31,500.00, including cost of points. Points at 3.0% (loan costs) based on the full amount of the line of credit, were charged against the line of credit at the time the line of credit was established. Simple annual interest at 11.5% is charged against the amount borrowed. The total cost of the line of credit at the end of the first six months was _____.

A. Less than $3,275.00
B. Between $3,275.00 and $3,375.00
C. Between $3,376.00 and $3,475.00
D. More than $3,475.00

A project currently in progress has had costs to date of $33,160.00. The total estimated costs for the completed project is $42,180.00. The amount billed to date is $36,870.00. The contract price for the project is $51,670.00. Calculate the % completion for this project.

64.2%
78.6%
87.4%
90.0%

A project currently in progress has had costs to date of $28,205.00. The estimated cost to complete the project is $11,410.00. The amount billed to date is $38,170.00. The contract price for the project is $31,500.00. What is the amount of "unearned" income?

0
$1,445.00
$1,503.00
$2,007.00

A contractor is planning to enter a new (different) construction market. In this market a few customer will account for the bulk of the business. The contractor's former business success has relied on many small accounts. Which of the following statements could be true of this situation?

A. A bad debt or customer loss in the new business could be difficult to absorb
B. A high yields in the new business could drop the overall yield
C. A large volume of new business with a percentage of profits equal to that of the old business could result in a lower overall yield on investment
D. The higher the risk of the new business the lower the yield should be

14) Which of the following statements is false?

A. Only the trend of bad debts needs to be known in order to control accounts receivable
B. The reserve for bad debts is a reduction in current assets
C. The estimate of available cash can be totally wrong without a good projection of bad debt loss
D. The older an outstanding debt becomes, the more likely it is to become a bad debt

15) In terms of profit, which of the following statements is false?

A. Success in increasing the margin of profit rests on the control of fixed expenses
B. Selling expenses usually rise in steps and are related to the volume of business
C. Fixed expenses tend to follow sales volume at the same rate
D. As volume and cash profits increase, some contractors tend to relax their control over selling expenses

1 Exam Prep – Builder's Guide to Accounting 5

16) When clarifying overhead expenses, which of the following would not be considered a fixed expense?

Postage
Telephone
Travel and Entertainment
Advertising and Promotion

A contracting company had initial organizational costs of $6,470.00. These costs are being amortized over a five-year period. For purposes of amortization, the organizational expenses were first entered into the company's books on January 1st, 2000. The asset amount that should be listed in the books for organizational expenses as of January 1, 2003 is _____.

$107.83
$2,588.00
$3,882.00
$6,470.00

A contractor purchased a piece of equipment for use in his/her business for a total price of $18,000.00. The equipment will have a useful life of five years and a salvage value of $1,500.00. Maintenance and repair costs will average $120.00 per month and costs of storage, insurance and taxes will average $90.00 per month. The contractor will use the equipment for projects on an average of 140 hours per month. The hourly cost for this piece of equipment when assigned to a specific project is _____ . Do not include labor, gas, oil or any other costs not given above.

A. Less than $3,40 per hour
B. Between $3.40 and $3.50 per hour
C. Between $3.51 and $160 per hour
D. More than $3.60 per hour

19) A complete cash plan does not:

A. Allow for seasonal business fluctuations
B. Prevent over or under buying of materials
C. Allow errors in cash planning and direction
D. Prepare for tax liabilities

20) The method of preparing a cash budget or forecast which involves budgeting only cash flow of actual cash in and out of a business is known as the _____.

A. Source and application of funds method
B. Gross margin method
C. Current ratio method
D. Cash movement method

21) A contractor who is preparing a cash budget can determine the minimum volume of business necessary to avoid a loss if the contractor knows the _____.

A. Available cash (only)
B. Total overhead (only)
C. Break even point
D. Trend in charge sale

22) Which of the following is not a sub-contract category for deferred costs and expenses?

Materials
Direct labor
Taxes
General Expenses

23) The best control and documentation method for use for petty cash is the _____.

A. Cash receipt method
B. Inprest system
C. Ledger system
D. Budgeted account method

24) Which of the following statements concerning a petty cash fund is true?

A. All expenses for a petty cash fun should be "vouched" for by replacing cash removed with a slip of paper explaining the reason for the expense
B. A well controlled petty cash fund will always have a positive balance
C. Expenses paid for through a petty cash fund cannot be deducted for tax purposes
D. A large amount of cash should be kept in the petty cash fund to anticipate any cash needs

The following information is available from the bank statement and the company checkbook at months end:

Bank statements ending balance: $47,705.00
Checkbook ending balance: $47,972.00
Bank service charges shown in the bank statement, but not entered in the checkbook totaled: $47.00
Outstanding checks that had not cleared the bank as of the close of the bank statement totaled: $2,150.00
The bank statement disclosed that a check recorded in the checkbook for $2,190.00 was actually made out for $1,290.00.
Deposits totaling $3,270.00 that had been entered in the checkbook had not been received prior to the closing date for the bank statement.

After reconciliation, the checkbook would show a balance of _____.

$47,705.00
$47,878.00
$48,332.00
$48,825.00

26) Expenses recorded earlier than the payment referred to as _____.
Accruals
Deferrals
Prepaid assets
Unearned debts

27) Deferred costs and expenses are classified balance sheet as _____.

A. Deferred debts
Deferred
Long term liabilities
Long term assets

28) A profit and loss statement shows that net profit is the amount remaining after the total expenses have been subtracted from the _____.

A. Working Capital
Assets
Gross Profit
Direct Costs

Part 2

1. Which of the following is considered a company's asset?

   A. Debts owed by the company
   B. Cash holdings of the company
   C. Accounts payable
   D. A financial liability

2. The financial statement showing the owner's equity in a business is referred to as the _____.

   A. Balance sheet
   B. Profit and loss statement
   C. Summary of operations
   D. B and C are correct

3. The income statement is also sometimes called _____.

   A. A balance sheet
   B. The profit and loss statement
   C. A statement of cash flow
   D. The general ledger

4. Payments received but not yet earned are referred to as income.

   A. Loss   B. Profit   C. Accrued   D. Unearned

   Given: A construction project's cost as of September 30th 2008 is $34,261 the total estimated costs (at completion) are $43,832.

   The contract price for the project is $54,466 and the amount billed as of September 30th 2008 is $41,794.

   As of September 30th 2008, using the percent completion method, the revenue recognized in exABCs of the amounts billed for this project were _____.

   A. $763   B. $2,038   C. $4,004   D. $7,533

6. The following financial information is available for a job in. progress September 30th 2008.

TOTAL CONTRACT PRICE	BILLINGS TO DATE	COST TO DATE	ESTIMATED COST TO COMPLETE
$1,655,400	$1,247,000	$1,264,000	$233,600

   As of September 30, 2008, the percent completion of this project was _____.

   A. 71.0%   B. 78.6%   C. 85.0%   D. 89.8%

1 Exam Prep – Builder's Guide to Accounting

Given: On one of a construction company's project costs to date are $28,210 the total estimate cost at completion is $38,463. The contract price for the project is $48,964 and the amount billed to date is $28,305. The percent completed for this project is _____ .

A. 57.6%   B. 67.8%   C. 73.3%   D. 99.4%

8. You billed the owner $57,060 which includes a 10% retainage. The contract amount is $253,600. You estimate the job is one third complete. Your unearned or accrued income would be _____ .

A. $27,473 unearned
B. $27,473 accrued
C. $21,133 unearned
D. $21,133

9. Income earned but payment not yet received is referred to as _____ income.

A. Lost   B. Profit   C Accrue   D. Unearned

A construction contract which will last 48 months has an expected total profit of $620,000. Profits will be realized evenly over the term of the contract. Using the percent completion method of accounting, the third year's net profit would be _____ .

A. 0   B. $155,000   C. $465,000   D. $620,000

11. When using the cash method of accounting _____ .

A. Income and expenses are recorded at the time that they are earned or incurred.
B. Income and expenses are recorded at the time they are received or paid.
C. Gives a company more timely financial picture.
D. Give a company a more accurate financial picture.

12. Which of the following statements is false?

A. The older an outstanding debt becomes, the more likely it is to become a bad debt.
B. Typically, it is better to write off bad debts as a tax loss at the end of the year than continue trying to collect the bad debt.
C. Bad debt losses have little or no effect on cash budgeting.
D. The reserve for bad debts reduABC working capital.

An analysis of a construction company's past financial performance shows that gross profit has been decreasing in relation to sales. Which of the following would not be a possible factor contributing to this?

A. Lack of control of material costs.
B. Increase in markup over costs.
C. Inventory losses.
D. Increase in idle time.

---

1 Exam Prep – Builder's Guide to Accounting

14. Given: The following information for projects completed in 2007.

Project Number	Revenue Direct	Direct Costs
103	$ 21,155	$ 12,451
104	$ 34,564	$ 27,517
105	$ 75,022	$ 68,103
106	$116,247	$109,262

Project number _____ contributed the most to the company's 2007 gross profit.

A. 103   B. 104   C. 105   D. 106

15. A debit memo from your bank could indicate _____ .

A. Interest accrued.
B. A check you wrote for $100 was cleared at $10.
C. A charge for printed checks.
D. None of these.

16. In the purchase journal the contractor's total charge purchases are treated as _____ .

A. Accounts payable.
B. Accounts receivable.
C. Inventory exclusions.
D. Accruals.

17. Purchase journals (for recording purchase orders) are best suited for _____ .

A. Inventory controls.
B. Checking the register.
C. Accounts payable source document.
D. None of these.

18. Which of the following is not a good method of valuing inventories to be charged to a job?

A. Specific cost.
B. First in-first out.
C. Last in-first out.
D. Job estimates.

Which cost basis valuation method for inventory assumes that the first materials purchased are the first used?

A. Specific cost.
B. First in-first out.
C. Last in-first out.
D. Exact purchases price.

20. What is the ratio of Cost of Goods Sold to Average Inventory based on the following data:

Inventory Jan. 1, 2007		$ 15,760
Labor	$137,000	
Material Purchased	$183,500	
Other direct costs	$ 68,500	
Inventory Dec. 31, 2007		$12,340

A. 15.91/1   B. 17.9/1   C. 27.9/1   D. 29.9/1

---

1 Exam Prep – Builder's Guide to Accounting   11

21. The most useful ratio for checking inventory levels in relation to determining what you should do is _____.

A. Sales/average inventory.
B. Cost of goods sold/average inventory.
C. Material purchased/ average inventory.
D. Total direct cost/average inventory.

22. A current asset is expected to be convertible to cash within _____.

A. 1 month   B. 6 months   C. 1 year   D. 5 years

23. Which of the following is not depreciated?

A. office equipment   B. a truck   C. office building   D. land

A piece of equipment is purchased by ABC Contractors for $6,000. The equipment is to be depreciated over six (6) years. Which depreciation method will yield the smallest depreciation for the first two-(2) years?

A. 200% declining balance.
B. 150% declining balance.
C. 125% declining balance
D. Straight line

The job cost ledger for a project in progress shows the following information for completed site excavation work:

Superintendent: $3,050
General labor: $4,260
Equipment rental: $4,500
Dewatering: $3,800
Fuel: $1,200
Net profit from sale of soil $6,000

The total volume of material excavated was 12,300 cubic yards at an estimated cost of $2.10 per cubic yard. Based on the above information the estimated cost for the excavation was _____.

A. $ 180 too low
B. equal to the actual cost
C. $ 5,820 too high
D. $ 15,020 too high

According to the Builder's Guide to Accounting the best way for a small company to handle disbursements for small day-to-day expenses such as postage, C.O.D. deliveries and other expenses too small to write a check for is to _____.

A. Require employees to pay with their own money and reimburse them monthly.
B. Use only those vendors which extend credit.
C. Assign one individual to be responsible for payment and reimburse daily.
D. Set up a "petty cash" and voucher system with enough currency on hand to suit routine periodic needs, balancing and reimbursing the fund, periodically.

27. ABC Contractors receives their December 2007 bank statement:

The balance shown on the bank statement is $12,720.
A $300 charge against the account was incorrectly made by the bank. A $450 check was received by the bookkeeper on December 29, 2007 when it was deposited into the ABC account.
Outstanding checks totaled $2,740 as of December 31, 2007.
Deposits not posted by December 31, 2007 were $4,280.
Service charge for the month was $22.
An "uncollected funds" charge was $20.
ABC checkbook balance is $14,602 on December 31, 2007.

The actual balance as of December 31, 2007 is _____.

A. unable to be computed without additional information.
B. $14,602 is the correct balance.
C. $14, 560 is the correct balance.
D. $15,010 is the correct balance.

28. Prepaid insurance is carried as a/an _____ on the Balance Sheet.

A. liability   B. fixed asset   C. asset   D. capital

29. Given XYZ Corporation's balance sheet:

Cash	$10,000
Accounts payable	$ 2,500
Contracts payable	$ 1,700
Note payable	$ 3,600
Other liabilities	$ 87,500
Accounts receivable	$ 3,000
Inventory	$ 7,000
Other assets	$ 97,500

What is the corporation's net worth?

A. $18,800   B. $20,060   C. $21,500   D. $22,200

30. The balance sheet showing the financial status of the company _____ while the profit and loss statement measures the expense versus return _____ .

A. over a period of time----- over a period of time.
B. over a period of time----- on a specific date.
C. on a specific date -----over a period of time
D. on a specific date -----on a specific date.

31. Given: Direct costs $ 137,500
            Gross sales $ 250,000
            Selling expenses $ 56,000

Based on this information the gross profit is and the net income is

  $98,000--$46,000
  $33,000--$23,500
  $112,500--$56,500
  $112,500--$66,250

32. A construction company has an estimated income (sales) of $300,000 for 2007. In order to achieve a gross profit ratio of 45% the cost of goods sold should be _____.

A. $135,000   B. $165,000   C. $195,000   D. $205,000

33. Refer to the balance sheet shown below:

BALANCE SHEET AS OF SEPTEMBER 30, 2008

ASSETS		LIABILITIES	
Cash	$ 5,100	Accounts payable	$35,540
Accounts receivable	$50,075	Current liabilities	$41,540
Current assets	$61,575	Long term debt	$16,000
Property and equipment	$28,225		
Total Assets	**$95,000**	**Total Liabilities**	**$58,540**

During the month of October 2008 the net effect of all business operations was:
  Cash increased $9,240
  Accounts receivable decreased $4,481
  Current liabilities acid long term debt increased $725
  The net worth of the company at the end of October 2008 is _____.

A. $25,014   B. $26,464   C. $35,426;   D. $37,494

34. Refer to the balance sheet shown below:

CURRENT ASSETS

Cash		$ 38,800.38
Accounts receivable	$ 53,850.73	
Reserve for bad debt	$ 899.78	
Net accounts receivable		$ 52,950.95
Inventory		$ 24,783.16
Total Current Assets		$116,534.49

CURRENT LIABILITIES Total Current Liabilities $110,543.77

What is the "quick ratio" for this company?

A. 0.81 B. 0.83 C. 0.89 D. none of these

Based on the balance sheet of problem 38, how much cash must be added to the assets to increase the "quick ratio" to 1.25.

A. $44,689.13 B. $46,428.38 C. $47,867.45 D. none of these

Questions 36 through 38 use the following data:

	COMPANY			
	A	B	C	D
Current assets	180,000	220,000	110,000	200,000
Total assets	410,000	480,000	360,000	460,000
Current liabilities	110,000	120,000	50,000	130,000
Total liabilities	340,000	360,000	310,000	410,000
Net income	21,000	23,000	14,000	24,000
Total sales	1,050,000	1,250,000	350,000	1,350,000

36. Which of the above companies has the largest current ratio?

A. company A
B. company B
C. company C
D. company D

37. Which company has the greatest margin of profit?

A. company A
B. company B
C. company C
D. company D

38. Which company has the greatest amount of working capital?

A. company A
B. company B
C. company C
D. company D

An unsecured contract is payable to Bank One in monthly payments of $744.00 plus simple interest at 11% per annum on the unpaid balance. The balance due as of December 31, 2007 was $13,392.00. How much of the January 2008 loan payment to Bank One was for interest?

A. $122.76 B. $344.03 C. $744.00 D. $982.08

Part 3

1. In a petty cash system, you_____ for all expenses by replacing cash removed with a_____.

   A. account - daily log
   B. vouch - slip of paper
   C. account - journal
   D. vouch – voucher

Most builders need a cash fund for the little expenses that come up from day to day such as_____.

   expenses less than $100
   expenses less than $75
   coffee and donuts, C.O.D. deliveries, and postage due
   accounts receivables less than $200

Controlling your overhead expenses is important, therefore your record of _____ is the best indication of what you can expect in the future.

   accounts receivables
   future expenses
   fixed overhead expenses
   past overhead expenses

4 Entries into the bookkeeping system for bills received but not yet paid are called_____ entries.
   accrual
   prepaid expenses
   deferral
   cash accounts

Financial and operating ratios are useful to builders and contractors who understand their meaning. These ratios tell the _____ trend of your business.

   day-to-day
   week-to-week
   month-to-month
   year-to-year

_____ help you find the good and the bad situations and show the relative health of your business.

   accounts payable
   accounts receivables
   chart of accounts
   ratios

The account entry to record accounts receivable is _____.

    defer the account
    credit the account
    debit the account
    accrue the account

In order for the general ledger to be correct it must _____.

    have the debit side greater than the credit side
    be balanced
    have a positive balance on the credit side
    have the credit side greater the than debit side

Which of the following formulas is correct regarding a balance sheet?

    liabilities + net worth = assets
    assets = net worth - liabilities
    assets = liabilities - net worth
    assets = liabilities ÷ net worth

The _____ shows the source of funds and summary of cash management.

    check register
    income statement
    balance sheet
    cash flow statement

A contractor has received a payment of $41,199 on a job which he is 35% complete. The payment represents 62% of the total contract. Based on the percentage method of accounting, what is the unearned income?

    $17,942
    $23,257
    $32,184
    $66,450

The advantage of using percentage of completion versus the completed contract method of accounting is _____.

    income and profits are based on estimates
    you can recognize income before a payment is received
    allows for periodic financial statements
    results in deferred income and profit

The method of accounting almost always used for small jobs and any other job of short duration is _____.

- accrual method
- unearned income method
- completed contract method
- percentage of completion method

Assume that a contractor had several moderate and ongoing large contracts underway. Which method of accounting will distort the true financial picture over several monthly accounting periods?

- accrual method
- unearned income method
- completed contract method
- percentage of completion method

A contractor is using the "completed contract method" of accounting. Under this method and according to Builder's Guide to Accounting, income is received when _____.

- an application for payment is made
- the project is completed
- an application for payment is made based on the percentage of completion of the total contract price
- D. at the owners' discretion and if the project is at least 75% complete

The method of accounting for long duration projects is _____.

- accrual method
- cash method
- completed contract method
- percentage of completion method

There are two accepted ways to record income. When comparing these two methods it is found that financial statements are not realistic under the _____ method of accounting.

- contract
- percentage of completion
- completed contract
- combined accounting

An alternative accrual method for builders is called the cash method. Under cash accounting, entries are made and reported only when _____.

   checks are written
   cash changes hands
   cash is received daily
   logged in journal

An aging list of accounts receivables not only shows you how long it is taking to collect account receivables but also _____.

   the amount of working capital at hand
   the amount of cash tied up in receivables (excluding retainages)
   the amount of cash tied up in inventory
   what percentage of total receivables are past due (excluding retainages)

What is the trend in the average length of receivables for a company given the following information:

Month	Avg. Receivables	12 Mo. Charge Sales
April	$32,518.00	$350,116.00
May	$28,267.00	$286,300.00
June	$30,112.00	$290,482.00

A. the average length of receivables is fluctuating
B. the average length of receivables is increasing
C. the average length of receivables is decreasing
D. the company's net worth is increasing

A bill for $3,000 was received by a contractor with an invoice date of June 10th. Terms of the agreement are, 2% discount if paid within 10 days of the invoice date, net 30. The bill was paid by the contractor on June 19th of the same month. The correct check amount should be _____.

   $3,000.00
   $2,904.00
   $2,940.00
   $2,490.00

How does a business get their credit customers to pay faster?

   by controlling the average days of outstanding receivables
   by offering invoice discounts such as: "2% - 10 days, net 30"
   by preparing and mailing monthly statements regularly
   by assigning the accounts receivables over to a professional collection agency

1 Exam Prep – Builder's Guide to Accounting

For estimating bad debt losses, you need only the _____ and bad debt losses for a two-year period.

> total credit sales
> bad debt reserve
> journal entries
> total delinquent sales

What should be done with bad debts at the end of the year?

> write them off if they are over 30 days delinquent
> credit the revenue account
> credit the expense account
> adjust accounts receivables for bad debts

The journal entry to record an uncollectable bad debt is _____.

> debit bad debt expense
> credit reserve for bad debts
> debit accounts receivable
> credit accounts receivable

The older an outstanding balance becomes, the more likely it is to become a/an _____.

> bad debt
> account receivable
> delinquent payable
> reserve for bad debt

When summarizing a company's bad study report, which of the following would indicate a favorable trend?

> delinquent receivables are increasing
> the ratio of delinquent receivables to total receivables are decreasing
> delinquent receivables remain the same while bad debts increase
> delinquent receivables and bad debts remain the same while credit sales decrease in relation to total sales

A contractor must control his accounts receivable. To do so, he only needs to know the trend of his _____.

> credit sales
> delinquent account
> bad debts
> bad debts and credit sales

The reserve for bad debts account is a reduction of your _____ and should appear in the general ledger immediately after the accounts receivable.

    current liabilities
    current assets
    cash flow
    fixed assets

A contractor is considering entering a new market with only a few customers. This new market will account for the bulk of his business. Which of the following is most correct?

    one bad debt or customer loss could hurt the business bad
    more volume would create a larger profit
    a good idea since overhead will not increase much
    bad debts or customer losses could be absorbed

What will the sales price need to be for a contractor to make a 10% gross profit on a job with total direct costs of $437,000?

    $473,595
    $480,350
    $485,556
    $490,800

You are putting a bid together using the information listed below. After submitting your bid to the owner, he counters your bid by saying he can only afford to pay $79,000 for the job. If you accept his counter offer and the job, what will be your net profit?

    Subcontractors bids $40,000
    Labor estimate $20,000
    Material estimate $8,000
    Indirect expenses on labor 8%
    Profit mark-up 10%

    $2,440
    $6,960
    $9,400
    $11,000

Selling expenses usually rise in steps and are related to the volume of business. As volume and cash profits increase, some builders _____.

    tend to relax their control over fixed expenses
    budget their accounts payable
    relax their control of petty cash
    tend to relax their control over selling expenses

In construction projects, which of the following is not the largest direct cost to a builder?

    material costs
    subcontracts
    labor costs
    cost of general conditions

According to *Builder's Guide to Accounting*, materials comprise approximately what percent of direct costs?

    8% to 10 %
    25%
    50%
    60%

The labor costs of moving materials from the curb line to the installation point on residential projects is estimated to be about _____.

    A. 4% to 6%
    B. 8% to 10%
    C. 15% to 17%
    D. 23% to 25%

The most simplest method of controlling material handling and scheduling is by _____.

    delivery schedules
    purchase orders
    controlling costs
    controlling inventory

The best way to provide control of materials entering your storage yard from vendors is by _____.

    A. signing and keeping copies of invoices
    B. performing weekly inventory
    C. making sure it gets unloaded when materials arrive
    D. summarizing your purchase orders on a purchase journal

Some builders use the purchase journal as a source document for accounting entries. The total purchases are treated as _____.

    credits
    accounts receivables
    debits
    accounts payable

According to *Builder's Guide to Accounting,* the real usefulness of a purchase journal is _____.

> to control accounts receivable
> to control accounts payable
> to control the bad debts of a company
> to control inventory

Lack of planning and controlling your inventory can leave you with too much material at any given time. This ties _____ up that could be better used.

> inventory
> material
> working capital
> labor

There are various methods of controlling inventory. Under one of the methods, the latest materials purchased are the first ones used. This method of keeping inventory is referred as _____.

> first in, first out
> specific cost
> last in, first out
> first in, last out

According to *Builder's Guide to Accounting* good inventory control does which one of the following?

> reduces the need for office space
> maximizes investments of capital inventory
> minimizes obsolescence losses
> helps avoid construction litigation

According to *Builder's Guide to Accounting,* what is the suggested method to avoid payroll problems?

> use double-stub payroll checks
> issue all checks from one general account
> established a separate payroll checking account
> use the pegboard system to write payroll checks

1 Exam Prep – Builder's Guide to Accounting   23

Which copy of the W-2 wage and tax statement should be given to the employee to file with his/her income tax return?

    Copy A
    Copy B
    Copy C
    Copy D

According to *Builder's Guide to Accounting*, the form required for depositing federal *FICA* and *witholding taxes* with local banks is _____.

    Form 8109
    Form 940
    Form 941
    Form 508

According to *Builder's Guide to Accounting*, which one of the following is not a variable expense?

    payroll taxes on direct labor
    property taxes
    job site equipment rental
    travel and entertainment

Which one of the following is true, when setting up a plan for budgeting overhead expenses?

    budgeting controls accounts receivable
    budgeting reduces the bidding process
    controls the accounts payable
    budgeting should be based on past results and your estimate of reasonable expectations

A monthly budget for fixed expenses should be prepared _____ in advance.

    60 days
    6 months
    1 year
    2 years

According to *Builder's Guide to Accounting*, using the accrual method of accounting, how often should a contractor make entries in the general ledger?

    weekly
    every two weeks
    monthly
    every six months

Every contractor should keep good purchasing records of equipment. In addition to these good records a contractor should develop detailed records for _____.

    operators who use the equipment
    brake horsepower of equipment
    equipment deprecation
    yearly cost of equipment operators

Every builder should keep certain information to establish an hourly cost of his equipment. Such information should be _____.

    hourly cost of equipment operator
    repair and maintenance depreciation
    cost of equipment minus estimated salvage value
    estimated life of each driver

According to *Builder's Guide to Accounting,* which of the following is *not* a unit cost of equipment?

    A. salvage value
    B. purchase price
    C. cost of storage
    D. idle time

A piece of equipment was purchased new for $5,000 and sold two years later for $3,350, using 15% straight line annual depreciation of acquisition cost, the net gain or loss on the sale is a _____. Assume a 7 year useful life.

    gain of $350.00
    loss of $150.00
    gain of $150.00
    loss of $350.00

According to the Modified Accelerated Cost Recovery System (MACRS), office furniture has a depreciable life class of _____.

    3 years
    5 years
    7 years
    10 years

The decision to buy equipment can be a major step for any contractor. One of the advantages of leasing equipment is _____.

- on a long term basis, leasing is cheaper
- an immediate tax deduction is available
- depreciation can begin immediately
- on a short-term basis, buying is cheaper

According to *Builder's Guide to Accounting,* which of the following statements is correct regarding leasing of equipment?

A. lease-purchased equipment is carried as an asset on financial statements even though offsetting liabilities are not included.
B. in the short term, owning is cheaper than leasing
C. for equipment that will receive regular long-term use, leasing is cheaper than buying
D. depreciation can be claimed on equipment that is leased-purchased

Under a lease purchase agreement, which one of the following is not true?

- full value of the equipment is included as an asset
- depreciation is not allowed
- the full liability less equity is listed as payable
- depreciation on the equipment can begin immediately

When equipment is sold, the books have to be cleared of all entries relating to that asset. This includes taking out the _____ of the asset and the _____ on it.

- market value - organizational expense
- accumulated depreciation - net value
- gross value - accumulated appreciation
- gross value - accumulated depreciation

A complete cash budgeting plan does much more than simply budget a certain amount of cash for a specific future use. It also _____.

- raises immediate cash
- liquidates current assets
- allows for bonds to be sold
- prevents errors in cash planning and direction

There are several ratios you can use to judge your cash position. They are called _____ and indicate the relative asset strength of a business.

- cash movement ratios
- cash control ratios
- liquidity tests
- leveraging ratios

The cash movement method and the source and application of funds method are two principle methods of preparing a cash budget. The cash movement method involves budgeting only the _____.

    accounts payable
    accounts receivable
    source of application
    flow of cash

According to *Builder's Guide to Accounting*, a good cash planning budget can accomplish_____.

    controlling the purchase of materials and helps prevent under- or over-buying
    preparation for tax assets
    planning adequate levels of purchasing in advance
    serving as a model for control of accounts payable

A contractor wants to improve the current ratio on it's balance sheet. How is this done?

    increasing current assets
    increasing net worth
    decreasing long-term liabilities
    decreasing current liabilities

There are several ratios a company can use to judge its cash position. One of those ratios is _____.

    expenses to sales
    income to net profit
    current liabilities to capitalization
    current assets to long-term liabilities

When preparing a cash budget, which method is especially valuable for builders who have wide variations in their business volume from month to month?

    cash budgeting method
    pegboard system
    cash movement method
    source and application of funds method

Which of the following statements is the most correct concerning a cash movement budget?

    cash movement method recognizes accounts receivable
    cash movement method is not valuable for builders who have wide variations in business volume
    source of applications of funds method has the advantage of simplicity
    cash movement method involves budgeting only the flow of actual cash

There are two principal methods of preparing a cash budget or forecast: the cash movement method and the source and application of funds method. The source and application of funds method is _____.

    less accurate
    for wide variations of business volume
    more precise than the cash movement method
    based on actual cash flow

A break-even point does not encourage growth. It merely tells you the _____ you need to break even.

    minimum amount of direct costs
    minimum amount of gross profit
    minimum amount of sales
    amount of budgeting

C.A.M. Construction Co. wants to figure their gross sales break-even point. If their fixed overhead is $95,000 and the selling expenses are $150,000, what is their break-even point if cost of contracts is 60% of sales (revenue)?

    $245,000
    $612,500
    $545,800
    $925,395

A new construction company estimates it's fixed overhead to be $35,000, sales expenses of 19%, and direct costs of 55%. In order to break even during it's first year of operation, the company must achieve a total sales volume of _____. Select the closest answer.

    $77,778
    $184,210
    $155,850
    $134,615

A company wishes to break even in sales volume. The company has operating expenses of $29,000 and gross profit represents 30% of gross income. What is the total direct cost?

    $96,667
    $29,667
    $48,667
    $67,667

Cash can be stolen in different ways. Which of the following is not a way for a contractor to lose cash through theft from employees?

    adjusting the check book
    lapping
    double use of petty cash receipts
    recording cash sales

A crew has a performance standard ratio of 1.2 to 1. The crew is to be sent on a job that will require 80 standard man-hours. According to the crew's performance standard, how many man-hours will it take the crew to complete the job?

    96.0
    76.4
    66.7
    66.6

A 3-man construction crew has consistently had an average performance standard ratio of 1.2 to 1 (actual to standard). This crew is scheduled for a job with a predetermined performance standard time requirement of 98 man-hours. If the crew works at the 1.2 to 1 performance standard ratio, the total actual time the crew will work on the scheduled job is _____.

    39.2 crew-hours
    78.4 crew-hours
    117.6 crew-hours
    156.8 crew-hours

Which of the following is not a classification of a deferred cost or expense account?

    materials
    direct labor
    taxes
    general expenses (allocated)

Deferred income is neither a current nor a long-term liability. It is a _____.

    deferred debit
    deferred credit
    deferred accrual
    long term liability

According to *Builder's Guide to Accounting*, costs and expenses are neither current nor long term. On a balance sheet they are classified as _____.

    deferred income
    deferred debits
    deferred expenses
    deferred credits

The only reasonable way to assign fixed overhead expenses is in proportion to _____.

    total direct cost
    gross sales
    total direct labor hours
    total direct labor cost

Which of the following is true, regarding the use of a *job cost ledger?*

    the system provides useful information but is not practical
    the system is time consuming and burdensome
    materials and payroll expenses are posted directly to the job cost ledger as you write checks to pay bills
    you can see project-to-date costs and expenses and the system is practical and provides useful information

Which of the following is the best way to control petty cash?

    withhold cash from a bank deposit
    write out a check to "petty cash" as funds are needed
    set up an imprest system
    make the fund difficult to use

Controlling the flow of information for cash payments is not difficult with a/an_____.

    cash voucher
    imprest fund
    receipt
    petty cash system

You are reconciling your company checkbook against your bank statement. Your checkbook indicates a balance of $18,500. There was a $65.00 service charge on the statement. You note a check you had entered in your checkbook as $690.00, was actually written for $960.00. Outstanding checks not posted in statement: $950.00, deposits not posted in statement: $870.00. What is the checkbook balance?

    $18,165
    $18,085
    $17,885
    $17,215

The most important information for accurate bidding is _____.

    estimated wage rates
    current material prices
    cost records of jobs completed
    subcontractor bids

The builder who has kept up a _____ on all previous work and has made a good material take-off should have no trouble estimating the true material cost.

    square foot cost
    job cost card
    performance standard record
    labor cost

Every builder should add a contingency to cover unknown conditions in his estimate, this contingency should be added _____.

    A. after the profit markup
    B. in the material estimate only
    C. at the end of estimate, just before adding the profit
    D. in the labor estimate only

The best method for allocating overhead is on the basis of _____.

    total cost of job as a percentage of total sales
    total labor hours
    percentage of gross profit
    percentage of net profit

Assume that the total projected direct labor hours estimated for C.A.M. Construction Co. are 21,000 man-hours for next year (12 months). Job #9149 is estimated to require 7,000 man hours to complete, and will last eight months. What dollar amount should be charged to job #9149 every month to cover C.A.M. Construction's general and administrative expenses for next year? Select the closest answer. The total projected general and administrative expenses for next year (12 months) is $52,500.00.

    $2,188.00
    $6,563.00
    $8,940.00
    $17,500.00

The best time to control costs on a construction project is _____.

    whenever you approve invoice statements for payment
    monthly as the job progresses along
    within each phase of construction that has been assigned a budget
    immediately following the project review

_____ are expenses recorded earlier than the payment is made.

    deferred debits
    deferred credits
    accruals
    pre-paid assets

Other than for contracts, accruals are recorded to show accounts and taxes payable, prepaid assets, and any other _____ that you expect will result in cash changing hands in the future.

    non-cash exchange
    cash exchange
    transaction
    deferrals

All sales on accounts receivables should be _____ because no cash changes hands.

    deferred
    advertised
    depreciated
    accrued

Insurance policy not expensed out is carried on the asset side of balance sheet as _____.

    A. accruals too low
    B. accruals too high
    C. deferrals too low
    D. deferrals too high

Details of the changes in current assets and current liabilities would be found on the _____.

    source of application of funds budget
    cash movement budget
    balance sheet
    income statement

The _____ is a general indicator of the strength of a contractor's operation and how well his business is able to finance its commitments.

    income statement
    balance sheet
    cash flow statement
    source and application method

Which of the following statements is true regarding a trial balance sheet?

- total credits must equal total debits
- total debits must equal total accruals
- total accruals must equal total credits
- current assets must equal current liabilities

The first step in preparing financial statements at the close of an accounting period and after all entries have been posted in the general ledger, is to put together a _____.

- post ledger
- cash flow statement
- chart of accounts
- trial balance sheet

Current assets are liquid assets that can be reasonably turned into cash within _____.

- 12 months
- 8 months
- 6 months
- 1 month

Fixed assets are classified as fixed, because they can not be reasonably to be turned into cash within _____.

- 1 month
- 6 months
- 8 months
- 12 months

Current liabilities are liabilities that are payable within _____.

- 1 month
- 6 months
- 1 year
- 2 years

Liability amounts that are not payable within 1 year are entered on a builder's books as _____.

- long-term accruals
- long-term liabilities
- current liabilities
- deferred expenses

Assume a contractor obtained a four year note from a bank. Which portion of that note would be considered a current liability?

>   all 48 months
>   the first 36 months
>   the last 12 months
>   the first 12 months

When equipment is sold or abandoned, the _____ should be removed from the books on that asset.

>   accumulated depreciation only
>   gross value only
>   gross value and accumulated depreciation
>   market value

Which of the following will be listed as an intangible asset?

>   goodwill
>   furniture & fixtures
>   improvements
>   retainage

According to *Builder's Guide to Accounting* which of the following accounts will be affected by dividends paid?

>   Cash: current assets
>   Accounts payable: current liabilities
>   Retained earnings: net worth
>   Accumulated depreciation: fixed assets

>   1 & 2
>   1 & 3
>   2 & 3
>   3 & 4

Accounting ratios will interpret and draw attention to significant conditions and trends such as _____

>   A. general indicators of business health at a given time
>   show day-to-day business trends
>   cash budgeting
>   controlling selling expenses

According to *Builder's Guide to Accounting*, what is the preferred minimum current ratio for contractors?

    1 to 1
    2 to 1
    3 to 1
    4 to 1

The formula to compute current ratio is _____.

    assets ÷ liabilities
    current assets ÷ total liabilities
    fixed assets ± current liabilities
    current assets ÷ current liabilities

Which one of the following ratios best portray a company's immediate ability to pay current debts?

    current ratio
    quick assets ratio
    working capital ratio
    margin of profit ratio

Financial planners at 1 Exam Prep Co. will use _____ when determining the business's ability to meet it's short term obligations.

    quick ratio
    current ratio
    working capital
    profit margin

Current assets minus inventories, divided by current liabilities equal _____.

    quick ratio
    net quick ratio
    working capital
    real turn over

Current assets minus current liabilities equal _____.

    quick ratio
    net quick ratio
    working capital
    real turn over

The type of ratios that compare accounts on the income statement to accounts on the balance sheet are called _____.

    combined ratios
    balance sheet ratios
    income account ratios
    comparative ratios

What type of ratio is the *real turnover* ratio?

    a combined ratio
    a balance sheet ratio
    an income account ratio
    an expense control ratio

The ratio that indicates the number of times that inventory is replaced in one year is referred to as _____ ratio.

    current
    true investment yield
    expense control
    real turnover

Cost of sales divided by inventory at cost equal _____.

    cost of sales percent
    trend in charge sales
    net quick ratio
    real turn over

Which of the following best describes how a true investment yield ratio may be obtained from financial statements?

    net income divided by net worth
    gross sales divided by net profit
    gross profit divided by net profit
    owners equity divided by net profit

Gross profit divided by sales equal _____.

    percentage of net profit
    gross profit percent
    expense control percent
    margin of profit

Operating expenses divided by sales volume equal _____.

    percentage of net profit
    gross profit percent
    expense control percent
    margin of profit

Net income divided by sales equal _____.

    percentage of net profit
    gross profit percent
    expense control percent
    margin of profit

Use the following information to determine which company has the most working capital.

Company	1	2	3	4
Current Assets	$270,000	$160,000	$250,000	$198,000
Current Liabilities	$180,000	$100,000	$110,000	$115,000
Avg Length Receivables	45	23	20	30
Sales	$1,400,000	$965,000	$2,410,000	$110,000

    A. Company 1
    B. Company 2
    C. Company 3
    D. Company 4

According to the income statement for 1 Exam Prep. Construction Co., the gross profit margin Is _____. **Use Exhibit #1**

    10%
    27%
    35%
    37%

According to the financial documents given for 1 Exam Prep. Construction Company, the expense control ratio is _____. **Use Exhibit #1**

    14.2%
    14.7%
    22.3%
    20.8%

1 Exam Prep. Construction Company's margin of profit for the calendar year is _____. **Use Exhibit #1**

    7.4%
    9.9%
    12.3%
    15.5%

In order for 1 Exam Prep. Construction Co. to have a gross profit of 40%, the cost of contracts would need to _____. **Use Exhibit #1**.

    increase by $212,835
    decrease by $212,835
    increase by $1,702,674
    decrease by $1,702,674

1 Exam Prep. Construction Co. wishes to increase their sales in the next year following the year shown on Exhibit #1. They anticipate no increase in operating expenses for the next year, and wish the expense to sales ratio to be 20%. To achieve this, sales must be _____.
Use Exhibit #1

    $851,336
    $4,256,684
    $4,427,595
    $7,023,527

According to the financial information given, the current ratio for 1 Exam Prep. Construction Co. is _____. **Use Exhibit #2**

    1.39:1
    1.59:1
    1.75:1
    1.96:1

The quick ratio for 1 Exam Prep. Construction Co. is _____. **Use Exhibit #2**

    1.32:1
    1.46:1
    1.63:1
    1.79:1

The working capital for 1 Exam Prep. Construction Co. is _____. **Use Exhibit #2**

    $318,375
    $487,896
    $523,465
    $631,983

According to the financial information given in Exhibit #3, what is the percentage of total sales for the Remodeling Division of 1 Exam Prep. Construction Co.?

    28%
    37%
    45%
    55%

The gross profit percentage for the New Construction Division of 1 Exam Prep. Construction Co. is _____. **See Exhibit #3.**

    23.2%
    32.7%
    41.0%
    49.4%

The margin of profit for the Remodeling Division of 1 Exam Prep. Construction Co. is _____. **See Exhibit #3**

    23.2%
    49.4%
    2.4%
    29.3%

The operating expenses of the Remodeling Division of 1 Exam Prep. Construction Co. are _____ of the total operating expense. **See Exhibit #3**.

    20.2%
    29.4%
    43.6%
    57.3%

Refer to the Schedule of Contracts in Progress **(Exhibit #4)** to determine the percentage of completion on job #9135. This job is estimated to be _____ complete.

    37.8%
    40.0%
    41.5%
    70.8%

Job #9135 has _____ of accrued/unearned income to date. **Use Exhibit #4.**

    $3,293 accrued
    $3,293 unearned
    $69,375 accrued
    $69,375 unearned

The lift truck on **Exhibit #5** will depreciate _____ for the first year.

$5,400
$6,500
$8,100
$10,800

The backhoe listed on **Exhibit #5** will depreciate _____ for the first year.

$15,000
$17,500
$22,500
$30,000

A company traded its old computer for a new model at the end of two years. The old computer has a useful life of six years. The following information is pertinent to this transaction:

- Cost of old computer $6,000
- List price of new model $8,000
- Trade-in allowance for old computer $4,500

According to *Builder's Guide to Accounting*, to defer tax on gains or losses until the new computer is sold, the adjusted basis for depreciation of the new asset would be _____. Use straight-line depreciation and assume no salvage value.

A. $ 7,500
   $10,500
   $11,000
   $12,000

If the actual profits on a current job are too high at the beginning of the job schedule, it may indicate that you will _____.

finish the project late
make a smaller overall job profit
need to reschedule labor and material for later dates
finish the project early

If the profit curve on a current job do not do not swing up soon enough or fast enough at the beginning of the job schedule, it can mean that you will _____.

finish the project early
make a larger overall job profit
need to examine the estimate to determine why the job is on schedule
need to delay scheduled labor and material until later dates

What information would not be required on a loan application?

   an income statement for one year
   a federal income tax return for the previous year
   a cash flow statement
   a current balance sheet

Which of the following is true regarding the Small Business Administration?

   The SBA guarantees loans from private banks lending to small businesses
   The SBA lends money to all small businesses independently owned
   The SBA is the largest lender of loans in the United States
   The SBA does not require collateral

The balance sheet account entry for taxes payable is _____.

   long-term liability
   current liability
   fixed liability
   deferred expenses

A contractor established a $150,000 line of credit with a bank. When it was established, 2 points were charged on the full amount of the line of credit. Simple annual interest at 10.5% was charged against the amount borrowed. During the first 6 months, the average amount borrowed was $99,000. What was the total cost of the line of credit at the end of 6 months?

   $6,697.50
   $8,197.50
   $10,395.00
   $13,395.00

A contractor borrows $112,500 from a bank at 13% simple annual interest. Two points are deducted from the loan proceeds at closing. The annual percentage interest rate is _____. Interest payments are made monthly. The principle plus accrued interest are paid at the end of the loan period. The loan is for _____ months.

   13.0%
   13.27%
   13.34%
   13.76%

1 Exam Prep – Builder's Guide to Accounting

A contractor took a $75,000, 6-month, 12% simple interest rate construction loan from a bank. The bank required monthly payments of this interest-only loan and deducted a 2-point origination fee from the loan amount. How much will the monthly payments be?

$735.00
$750.00
$3,045.00
$9,000.00

A contractor took a $100,000, 9-month, 10% simple interest rate construction loan from a bank. The bank required monthly payments of this interest-only loan and deducted a 2-point origination fee from the loan amount. How much did the contractor pay the bank on the final payment?

$98,816.67
$100,000.00
$100,833.33
$107,500.00

EXHIBIT #1
INCOME STATEMENT

Income:

    Construction income (sales) $4,256,684

    Cost of contracts $2,766,845

    Gross profit $1,489,839

Operating expenses:

    Selling expenses $ 359,824

    General & administrative expenses:

        Salaries $ 433,195

        Utilities $ 13,000

        Office $ 37,000

        Insurance $ 18,000

        Miscellaneous $ 24,500

Total operating expenses: $ 885,519

Operating profit: $ 604,320

Net income before taxes: $ 604,320

    Taxes $ 181,996

Net income: $ 422,324

EXHIBIT #2 BALANCE SHEET

Current assets:

Cash in bank	$	198,357
Petty cash		1,000
Accounts receivable		965,368
Materials in inventory		107,641
Prepaid items		38,000

Total current assets: $ 1,310,366

Fixed assets:

Equipment & machinery	$	450,000
Building & improvements		965,258
Accumulated depreciation		(143,000)

Total fixed assets: $ 1,272,258

Total assets: $ 2,582,624

Current liabilities:

Accounts payable	$	583,259
Notes payable		163,852
Payroll taxes payable		75,359

Total current liabilities: $ 822,470

Long term liabilities:

Notes & mortgages		422,453
Total liabilities	$	1,244,923

Capital (net worth):

Capital stock		150,000
Retained earnings		765,377
Net income (year-to-date)		422,324

Total capital: $ 1,337,701

Total liabilities & capital: $ 2,582,624

EXHIBIT #3
PROFIT AND LOSS STATEMENT

	Total	Less: New Construction	Remodeling Only
Gross income:	$ 4,256,684	$ 2,341,176	$ 1,915,508
Direct cost:	2,766,845	1,798,449	968,396
	100%		
Gross profit:	$ 1,489,839	$ 542,727	
Operating expenses:			
Selling expenses	359,824	210,731	149,593
G & A expenses	525,695	288,857	236,338
Total operating expenses	$ 885,519	$ 499,588	$ 385,931
Net profit:	$ 604,320	$ 43,139	$ 561,181
Margin:	_____	_____	_____

1 Exam Prep – Builder's Guide to Accounting   45

EXHIBIT #4
SCHEDULE OF CONTRACTS IN PROGRESS

Project Number	Total Contract	Billings to Date	Estimated Cost to Date	Estimated Cost To Complete
9134	$175,000	$100,000	$90,000	$58,000
9135	225,000	90,000	85,000	120,000
9136	120,000	40,000	30,000	76,000
9137	125,000	52,000	40,000	60,000
9138	350,000	265,000	275,000	90,000
9139	500,000	460,000	450,000	40,000
9140	138,000	20,000	20,000	115,000
9141	55,000	12,000	10,000	38,000
9142	985,000	980,000	1,100,000	5,000
	$2,673,000	$2,019,000	$2,100,000	$602,000

EXHIBIT #5
EQUIPMENT SCHEDULE

Depreciation	Description	Purchase Date	Purchase Price	Useful Life
Straight Line	Car	05/18/94	25,000	3 years
200% Declining Balance	Lift truck	08/28/95	27,000	5 years
150% Declining Balance	Back-hoe	11/07/95	150,000	10 years
150% Declining Balance	Pay loader	06/19/95	220,000	7 years

ANSWER KEY

Part 1

D

Step 1: Determine the cost of the materials including tax:
$9,200 x .06 (6%) = $552.00 tax
$9,200 + $552 = $9,752 total cost of materials

Step 2: Determine the job overhead cost (42% of labor cost):
$6,700 (labor) x .42 (42%) = $ 2,814

Step 3: Add the following figures:
Subcontractors: $37,500
Labor Costs: $6,700
Materials: $9,752
Job Overhead: $2,814
$37,500 + $6,700 + $9,752 + $2,814 = $56,766
Note: $56,766 is total price of bid before factoring the mark-up and bond.

Step 4: Determine the mark-up on the bid:
$56,766 x .08 (8%) = $4,541.28
$56,766 + $4,541.28 = $61,307.28
Note: $61,307.28 is total price of bid before factoring the bond.

Step 5: Determine the bond on the bid (.75% of total bid price after mark-up):
$61,307.28 x .075 (.75%) = $459.8046
$61,307.28 x $459.8046 = $61,767.084
Total BID Price is: $61,767.00 rounded to nearest dollar

 C
 CPage 269
 B
 C
 B
 C
 D
 C
 B
 B
 C
 A
 A
 C
 C

---

1 Exam Prep – Builder's Guide to Accounting

B
B
C
D
C
C
B
A
D
A
A
C

Part 2

B
A
B
D
A
C
C
B
C
B
B
C
B
A
B
A
A
D
B
C
B
C
D
D
D
D
C
C
D
C
C
B

1 Exam Prep – Builder's Guide to Accounting

D
B
B
C
C
B
A

Part 3

1.   D   10

Answer D is selected over B because a "slip of paper" is not necessarily a voucher and a voucher is not necessarily a "slip of paper". If Answer D was not among the choices Answer B would be satisfactory.

2.   C   10

3.   D   11

4.   A   11, 149

5.   C   12

6.   D   12

7.   C   15   chart (lower right)

8.   B   17, 278 or 281

9.   A   17

10.   D   18

11.   A   23 $41,199/.62 = 66,450
    66,450 x .35 = 23,257.50
    41,199 - 23,257.50 = $17,941.50

12.   B   24

13.   C   25

14.   C   25

15.   B   25

16.   D   26

17.	C	26	
18.	B	32	
19.	D	46	
20.	B	54, 55	32,518/350,116 x 365 = 33.52 days 28,267/286,300 x 365 = 36.04 days 30,112/290,482 x 365 = 37.84 days
21.	C	59	$3,000 x .98 = $2,940
22.	B	59	
23.	A	64	
24.	D	64	
25.	D	64	
26.	A	66	
27.	B	66, 67	
28.	D	67	
29.	B	68	
30.	A	80	
31.	C	82	Figure 7-4 100% - 10% = 90% (direct cost) 437,000/.90 = $485,555.56
32.	C	90	40,000 + 20,000 + 8,000 + (20,000 x .08) = 69,600 79,000 - 69,600 = $9,400
33.	D	91	
34.	D	115	
35.	C	115	

36.	B	115	
37.	B	116	
38.	D	118	
39.	D	118	
40.	D	118	
41.	C	119	
42.	C	120	
43.	C	121, 122	
44.	C	126	
45.	B	137	
46.	A	138	
47.	B	142, Figure 12-1 or 142 & 143	
48.	D	144	
49.	C	145	
50.	C	149 or 239	
51.	C	159	
52.	C	159, 160	
53.	A	159, 160	
54.	B	163, 170	5,000 x .15 x 2 =1,500 5,000 - 1,500 = 3,500 - 3,350 = $150 loss
55.	C	167	
56.	B	169	
57.	D	169, 170	
58.	B	169, 170	

1 Exam Prep – Builder's Guide to Accounting 51

#	Ans	Page	Work
59.	D	170	
60.	D	173	
61.	C	174	
62.	D	176	
63.	A	173, 174	
64.	D	174	
65.	A	175	
66.	C	176	
67.	D	176	
68.	C	176	
69.	C	178, 179	
70.	B	178, 179	100% - 60% = 40% (gross profit %) 95,000 + 150,000 = 245,000 (gross profit amount) 245,000/.40 = $612,500
71.	D	178, 179	100% - 55% = 45% (gross profit) 45% - 19% = 26% (fixed exp. %) 35,000/.26 = $134,615.38
72.	D	178, 179	100% - 30% = 70% (direct costs) 0 + 29,000 = 29,000 (gross profit) 29,000/.30 = 96,666.67 x .70 = $67,666.67
73.	D	180, 181, 182	
74.	A	189 & 190, Fig.15-3	80 x 1.2 = 96 man hours
75.	A	190	98 x 1.2 = 117.6 man hrs 117.6/3 = 39. 76. C 191
76.	C	191	

77.	B	191	
78.	B	191	
79.	C	201	
80.	D	203	
81.	C	207, 208	
82.	B	208	
83.	A	213, 214, 215	Check Book = 18,500 - 65 - 270 (960 - 690) = $18,165
84.	C	225	
85.	B	227	
86.	C	227	
87.	B	228	
88.	A	228, 229	52,500/21,000 = $2.50/hour x 7,000/8 = $2,187.50
89.	C	231	
90.	C	238	
91.	A	237	
92.	D	239	
93.	B	239, 240	
94.	C	247	
95.	B	249	
96.	A	250	
97.	D	250 or 281	
98.	A	252	
99.	D	252	

1 Exam Prep – Builder's Guide to Accounting

100.	C	253
101.	B	253
102.	D	253
103.	C	252, 253
104.	A	253
105.	B	254
106.	A	268
107.	B	268
108.	D	268 or 273
109.	B	269
110.	A	269
111.	A	269 or 273
112.	C	269 or 273
113.	A	270
114.	A	270 271 or 273
115.	D	271
116.	D	271 or 273
117.	A	272 or 273
118.	B	272 or 273
119.	C	272 or 273
120.	D	272 or 273
121.	C	273

Current Assets - Current Liabilities
1 = 270,000 - 180,000 = $90,000
2 = 160,000 - 100,000 = $60,00

1 Exam Prep – Builder's Guide to Accounting

			3 = 250,000 - 110,000 = $140,000
			4 = 198,000 - 115,000 = $83,000
122.	C	273	Gross profit/Sales 1,489,839/4,256,684 = .35 = 35%
123.	D	273	Operating Exp./Sales 885,519/4,256,684 = .208 = 20.8%
124.	B	273	Net income/Sales 422,324/4,256,684 = .099 = 9.9%
125.	B	general knowledge	4,256,684 x .40 = 1,702,673.60 -1,489 839 = $212,834.60 decrease
126.	C	general knowledge	885,519/.20 = $4,427,595
127.	B	273	Current Assets/Current Liabilities = 1,310,366/822,470 = 1.59 to 1.00
128.	B	273	Current Assets - Inventory/Current Liabilities 1,310,366 - 107,641/822,470 = 1.46 to 1.00
129.	B	273	Current Assets - Current Liabilities 1,310,366 - 822,470 = $487,896
130.	C	88, 89	1,915,508/4,256,684 = .45 = 45%
131.	A	273	542,727/2,341,176 = .232 = 23.2%
132.	D	273	561,181/1,915,508 = .293 = 29.3%
133.	C	88, 89	385,931/885,519 = .436 = 43.6%
134.	C	24	85,000/(85,000 + 120,000) = .415 = 41.5%
135.	A	23, 24	85,000/(85,000 + 120,000) x 225,000 =

1 Exam Prep – Builder's Guide to Accounting   55

			93,292.68 earned income — 90,000 = $3,292.68 accrued income
136.	D	164, 165	
			27,000/5 years x 2 (200%) = $10,800
137.	C	164, 165	
			150,000/10 years x 1.5 (150%) = $22,500
138.	A	163, 170	Original cost — accumulated depreciation = book value + new asset — trade-in = adjusted depreciation basis on new asset. Accumulated depreciation = 6,000/6 years x 2 = $2,000 6,000 — 2,000 = $4,000 (book value) + 8,000 — 4,500 = $7,500 = adjusted new basis for depreciation
139.	D	308	
140.	D	308	
141.	C	317	
142.	A	319	
143.	B	327	
144.	B	general knowledge	(150,000 x .02) + (99,000 x .105/12 x 6) = $8,197.50
145.	B	general knowledge	Annual percentage rate = Interest per year/net proceeds 112,500 x .13/112,500 x .98 = 14,625/110,250 = .1327 = 13.27%
146.	B	general knowledge	75,000 x .12/12 months = $750.00
147.	C	general knowledge	last payment due = principal due plus the last month of interest 100,000 x .10/12 = 833.33 + 100,000 = $100,833.33

1 Exam Prep – Builder's Guide to Accounting   56

1 Exam Prep
State Business and Finance
AIA A201-2017, A401-2017, A701-1997
Questions and Answers

The owner's right to carry out work begun by the contractor, but not completed, may occur after giving the contractor(s) _____ days notice.

    1
    10
    7
    12

A subcontractor may terminate a subcontract for non-payment of outstanding amounts due under the subcontract and late for _____ days.

    2
    30
    60
    90

The owner must prove financial capability no later than _____ days prior to the expiration of the time for withdrawal of bids.

    3
    5
    7
    30

Within _____ business days of the date the Contractor becomes aware of an impending or actual cancellation or expiration of any Contractor's insurance required by the contact documents, the Contractor shall provide notice to the owner.

    1
    2
    3
    4

Within _____ days after receipt of a written request, or earlier if so required by law, the Contractor shall furnish to the Subcontractor a copy of any bond covering payment obligations under the Subcontract Documents or shall authorize a copy to be furnished.

    45
    30
    15
    7

The architect has the sole responsibility for ordering _____.

- Change orders
- Construction change directives
- Any minor change in work
- Any changes whatsoever

Final payment, constituting the entire unpaid balance of the contract sum, shall be due when the work is fully completed and performed and the _____ has issued a certificate for payment.

- Architect
- Owner
- Builder
- Architect and owner

If the architect objects to the contractor's request for payment, he has _____ days to notify the contractor and owner.

- 7
- 10
- 14
- 21

Any changes or corrections of the bidding documents must be made by the _____.

- General contractor
- Addendum
- Certified mail
- Phone call

If within _____ of Substantial Completion, any of the work is found to be defective or not in accordance with the contract documents, the contractor shall correct it promptly after receipt of a written notice from the owner to do so.

- Six months
- One year
- Fifteen months
- Eighteen months

Given the following:

The architect of a construction project approved a shop drawing submitted and approved by the project's prime contractor but prepared by a subcontractor.

After the architect's approval, a deviation was discovered in the shop drawings when compared with the project plans and specifications.

2

According to AIA A201, the responsibility to correct the deviation lies with the _____.

- Owner
- Subcontractor
- Contractor
- Architect

If the subcontractor defaults or neglects to carry out the work in accordance with this agreement and fails after receiving written notice from the contractor to commence and continue correction of such default or neglect with diligence and promptness, the contractor may, after giving _____ days from the receipt by the subcontractor of any additional written notice, and without prejudice to any other remedy he may have, make good such deficiencies and may reduce the cost from the money owing to subcontractor.

- 2
- 3
- 5
- 7

The _____ shall be responsible for purchasing and maintaining required insurance of and limits of liability, and subject to the terms and conditions, as described in he Agreement or Contract.

- Architect
- Contractor
- Owner
- Mortgage

Given the following:

A change directive is issued by the architect for $2,100
The contractor did not respond promptly to the architect's change directive and does not agree with the architects cost and submits the following cost:
- Labor $ 825
- Materials $1,450
- Machinery rental $ 300
- Hand tool rental $ 400
   Contractor mark-up 15%

How much can the contractor expect to receive based on his cost estimates?

- 2,575
- 2,975
- 2,961
- 3,421

The subcontractor shall not assign or subcontract without the consent of the _____.

- Architect
- Owner
- Contractor
- Architect and owner

3

Allowances shall cover the cost to the contractor of all materials and equipment

- Delivered to the site, all taxes, less trade discounts
- Delivered to the site, all taxes, less trade discounts, contractor transportation, handling, installation, overhead, profit and other expenses
- Delivered to the site, all taxes, plus trade discounts, unloading, handling, installation, overhead, profit and other expenses
- Delivered to the site, all taxes, double discounts, unloading, handling, installation overhead, profit and other expenses

Given the following:

The contractor encounters a concealed physical condition on January 22 r4 that will cause the contract price to be adjusted
The contractor notifies the architect promptly before conditions at the site are disturbed on January 22nd
The architect examines the condition on February 3r d and determines that no change in the contract is justified

According to AIA document, A201, the contractor must make a written claim for adjustment by _____ .

A. February 24
B. February 16
C. February 21
D. April 4

18. According to AIA document A-401, within _____ days following issuance by the architect of the certificate for payment covering such substantially completed work, the contractor shall, to the full extent provided in the contract documents, make payment to the subcontractor of the entire unpaid balance of the contract sum or of that portion of the contract sum attributable to the substantially completed work.

- 10
- 15
- 20
- 30

19. AIA bids are received _____ .

A. In a sealed envelope
B. By phone — bidder to contractor
C. In a legal size envelope
D. All of the above

Which of the following documents are required to be on site for the owner?

- Drawings
- Specifications
- Change orders
- All of the above

21. According to AIA document A401, the subcontractor's ability to assign his position as the subcontractor is .

    A. Not permissible at any time
    B. Permissible with the written consent of the contractor
    C. May assign the contract only in a bankruptcy situation
    D. May not assign the contract unless an approval in writing is received the architect from

22. The following is a breakdown of cost for a construction project

    Plans $ 400
    Permit fee $2,950
    County $4,200
    Assessment $ 500
    Survey

According to the contract provisions found in AIA document A-201, the contractor is responsible for the payment of _____ .

    $400
    $2,950
    $3,350
    $8,050

23. According to AIA document A-401 the contractor shall pay the subcontractor each progress payment and the final payment within _____ days after he receives payment from the owner.

    3
    5
    7
    10

24. Allowances as defined by AIA Document A-201 shall cover _____ .

    A. The cost to the contractor of materials, equipment and delivery but not trade discount
    B. The cost to the contractor of materials, equipment and delivery and trade discounts
    C. Delivery, trade discounts, reasonable mark-up but not loading and unloading
    D. Only hard and soft costs

25. The subcontractor shall report within _____ day(s) to the contractor any injury to any of the subcontractors' employees at the site.

    A. 1
    B. 2
    C. 3
    D. 4

26. A change order must be signed by _____.

    A. Owner and contractor
    B. Architect and contractor
    C. Owner and architect
    D. Owner, architect and contractor

A subcontractor has the same responsibility and obligation to the contractor as the _____.

    Architect has to the owner
    Owner has to the contractor
    Owner has to the architect and contractor
    Contractor has to the architect and owner

The _____ may reject a subcontractor hired by the contractor.

    Architect
    Contractor
    Owner
    A and C are correct

The bidder shall deliver the required bonds to the owner not later than _____ days following the date of the execution of the contract.

    1
    3
    5
    7

A construction change directive provides for a change in cost or time. The cost may include all of the following except _____.

    Labor
    Materials
    Hand tools
    Bonds

Please see the answer key on the following page***

1 Exam Prep
State Business and Finance
AIA A201 -2017, A401- 2017, A701-1997
Answer Key

1.	B	2.5	A.I.A. 201
2.	C	7.1	A.I.A. 401
3.	C	6.2	A.I.A. 701
4.	C	11.1.4	A.I.A. 201
5.	B	3.3.7	A.I.A. 401
6.	C	7.1.2	A.I.A. 201
7.	A	11.3.1	A.I.A. 401
8.	A	9.4.1	A.I.A. 201
9.	B	3.2.3	A.I.A. 701
10.	B	12.2.2.1	A.I.A. 201
11.	C	3.12.8	A.I.A. 201
12.	C	3.5	A.I.A. 401
13.	C	11.2.1	A.I.A. 201
14.	C	7.3.4	A.I.A. 201
15.	C	7.4.2	A.I.A. 401
16.	A	3.8.2	A.I.A. 201
17.	A	15.1.3.1	A.I.A. 201
18.	D	11.2	A.I.A. 401
19.	A	4.3.1	A.I.A. 701
20.	D	3.11	A.I.A. 201
21.	B	7.4.2	A.I.A. 401
22.	B	3.7.1	A.I.A. 201
23.	C	11.1.3	A.I.A. 401
24.	A	3.8.2	A.I.A. 201
25.	C	4.3.1	A.I.A. 401
26.	D	7.2.1	A.I.A. 201
27.	D	5.3	A.I.A. 201
28.	D	5.2.2	A.I.A. 201
29.	B	7.2.1	A.I.A. 701
30.	C	7.3.7	A.I.A. 201

7

1 Exam Prep
AIA A701 - 2018
Questions and Answers

1. Written or graphic instruments used by the architect prior to the execution of the contract which modify or interpret the bidding documents by additions, deletions, clarifications or corrections are referred to as _____.

    amendment
    change order
    change directive
    addenda

A bidder by making a bid represents that _____.

    the bid is based on materials required by the bidding documents with exceptions
    bidder has posted a letter of credit
    the bidder has visited the site
    bidder has general liability insurance

A deposit may be required from a bidder who obtains complete sets of bidding documents from the issuing office. The deposit will be refunded to bidders who submit a bona fide bid and return the bidding documents in good condition within _____ days after receipt of bids.

    5
    10
    15
    30

Bidders and sub-bidders requiring clarification or interpretation of the bidding documents shall make a written request which shall reach the architect at least _____ days prior to the date for receipt of bids.

    7
    14
    21
    30

Interpretations, corrections and changes of the bidding documents will be made by _____.

    addendum
    change directive
    change order
    amendment

No substitution for materials, products or equipment will be considered prior to receipt of bids unless written request for approval has been received by the architect at least _____ days prior to the date for receipt of bids.

    30
    15
    10
    5

All copies of the bid, the bid security, if any, and other documents required to be submitted with the bid shall be enclosed in a sealed, _____ envelope.

    transparent
    opaque
    red
    blue

Oral, telephonic or telegraphic bids are _____ and will not receive consideration.

    invalid after 3 days
    valid for 24 hours
    invalid after 5 days
    invalid

At the discretion of the owner, if stipulated in the advertisement or invitation to bid, the properly identified bids received on time will be opened _____ and will be read aloud.

    publicly
    privately
    after 3 days
    after 24 hours

The owner shall, at the request of the bidder to whom award of a contract is under consideration and no later than _____ days prior to the expiration of the time for withdrawal of bids, furnish to the bidder reasonable evidence that financial arrangements have been made to fulfill the owners obligations under the contract.

    30
    21
    14
    7

If the bidding documents require either a performance bond or a payment bond, the cost shall_____.

> not be included in the change order
> be included in the change order
> be added later to the bid in determining the contract sum
> be included in the bid

The bidder making a bid represents that he or she _____.

> is familiar with local conditions under which the work is to be performed
> is making a bid contingent on standard codes and conditions
> will adjust accordingly if the bid is accepted as long as an addendum is made
> will provide specifications for all materials

The proposed contract documents consist of _____.

> The form of agreement between the owner and the contractor and instruction to bidders
> The conditions of the contract (general, supplementary and other conditions), drawings, specifications and all addenda
> Advertisement or invitation to bid, instructions to bidders, the bid form, and other sample bidding and contract forms
> All addenda or written, graphic instruments issued by the Architect prior to the execution of the contract

A contractor furnished a bid on a project according to the provisions of *AIA Document A701*. The bid was received and accepted by the owner after the designated time and date required on the bidding documents for the receipt of all bids. The bidding documents required that the contractor furnish a performance bond and a payment bond. The contractor did **not** furnish a performance bond and a payment bond and, also refused to enter into a contract with the owner and withdrew the bid. What damages, if any, can be assessed against the contractor by the owner?

> no penalty. A contractor can withdraw a bid at any time he/she chooses
> the amount of bid security shall be forfeited to the owner as liquidated damages, as a penalty
> a penalty equal to 2.0% of the bid price
> the amount of bid security shall be forfeited to the owner as liquidated damages, not as a penalty

An architect has issued addenda prior to bid due date. According to AIA Document A701, the architect must issue all addenda at least _____ days prior to date for receiving all bids.

> 4
> 6
> 8
> 10

The burden of proof of the merit for any proposed substitution of materials, equipment or products in the bidding documents is upon the _____.

    architect
    owner
    proposer
    supplier

During the bidding process, where there is a discrepancy in the drawings or specifications, any corrections shall be made by _____.

    instructions to bidders
    addendum
    change order
    change directive

A bidder discovers that there is a discrepancy between the plans and the specifications. The bidder should _____.

    report it to the owner within seven days written notice
    talk to the other bidders
    ignore it
    report it to the architect immediately

Any performance bond or payment bond required in the bidding documents shall be delivered by the bidder to the owner not later than _____ days following the date of execution of the contract.

    3
    5
    7
    10

The owner must prove financial capability no later than _____ days prior to the expiration of the time for withdrawal of bids.

    3
    5
    7
    30

Any changes or corrections of the bidding documents must be made by the _____.

    General contractor
    Addendum
    Certified mail
    Phone call

22. AIA bids are received _____ .

    A. in a sealed envelope
    B. by phone — bidder to contractor
    C. in a legal size envelope
    D. all of the above

The bidder shall deliver the required bonds to the owner not later than _____ days following the date of the execution of the contract.

    1
    3
    5
    7

The owner shall, at the request of the bidder to whom the award of a contract is under consideration, furnish reasonable evidence that financial arrangements have been made to fulfill the contract within how many days prior to expiration of the time for withdrawal of bids?

    3 days
    4 days
    7 days
    10 days

Bidders and sub-bidders requiring clarification of the bidding documents shall make a written request to the architect at least _____ days prior to the date for receipt of bids.

    3
    5
    7
    10

1 Exam Prep
AIA A701
Questions and Answers

1.	D	1.3
2.	C	2.1
3.	B	3.2
4.	A	3.2.2
5.	A	3.2.3
6.	C	3.3.2.1
7.	B	4.3.2
8.	D	4.3.5
9.	A	5.1
10.	D	6.2
11.	D	7.1.2
12.	A	2.1
13.	B	1.1
14.	D	4.2.2
15.	A	3.4.3
16.	C	3.3.3
17.	B	3.2.3
18.	D	3.2.1
19.	A	7.2.1
20.	C	6.2
21.	B	3.2.3
22.	A	4.3.2
23.	B	7.2.1
24.	C	6.2
25.	C	3.2.2

1 Exam Prep
2017 Contractors Manual
Questions and Answers - 1

1. Failure to properly maintain OSHA logs could result in a base penalty of _____ .

   $100
   $1,000
   $7,000
   $500

   The minimum number of employees that will require a contractor to obtain workmen's compensation insurance is _____ employee (s).

   one
   three
   four
   ten

   The type of bond that guarantees that the contractor will perform the work in accordance with the contract is known as a _____ Bond.

   Bid
   Payment
   Performance
   Stipulated

   A short term project schedule is a detailed explanation of the next two weeks of construction activities and should be developed and/or reviewed by all of the following except _____.

   superintendent
   architect
   subcontractors
   project engineer

5. The _____ usually prepares the project schedule.

   Architect
   Owner
   Project Manager
   Engineer

In order to provide adequate control, the project schedule should be formally reviewed and updated _____.

A. at the project commencement
B. at least once every 30 days
C. at least once every 6 months
D. at the project closeout

7. A contract will not be enforced if it is _____ .

   oral
   illegal
   no work is accomplished for 90 days
   all of the above

According to the Statute of Frauds, a contract need not be in writing and still be enforceable in Florida if _____ and _____.

A. less than $500 in value and less than 2 years in length
B. less than $1,000 in value and less than 1 year in length
C. less than $2,500 in value and less than 1 year in length
D. less than $500 in value and less than 1 year in length

9. The _____ has the duty to record and post a Notice of Commencement to improve real property

   owner
   agent
   contractor
   any of above

A subcontractor started work on his contract with the General Contractor on August 1, 1999. The owner made the final payment to the general Contractor on September 13, 1999. The latest date the subcontractor can serve notice to owner to preserve his claim under the Construction Lien Law is _____, 1999.

A. Sept. 16
B. Sept. 15
C. Sept. 13
D. Sept. 12

The type of contract where in the contractor agrees to carry out a stipulated job in exchange for a fixed sum of money is a _____ contract.

A. Cost plus fixed
B. Lump sum
   GMP
   Cost plus

When a contractor has to perform extra work for a subcontractor, he will recover the cost in the form of a _____.

A. change order
B. back charge
C. bond payment
D. addendum

13. The _____ should be jointly prepared with a material and equipment schedule.

A. project schedule
B. 1st payment request
C. bid proposal
D. schedule of values

Based on the completed contract method, for a job bid at $300,000 and currently 66.67% complete, with a gross profit of 16.67% ($50,000), the current amount of profit recognized would be _____ .

$200,000
$0
$50,000
$33,335

Prior to beginning a drug testing program, an employer shall ensure that at least _____ days elapse between the notice and the start of testing.

A. 30
B. 45
C. 60
D. 90

16. A lien that is properly perfected may be discharged by any of the following except _____.

A. the completion of the project
B. by failure to begin action to enforce within prescribed time limit
C. by an order of the circuit court
D. by recording in clerk's office of a judgment by court of competent jurisdiction

After relocating his business to a new location, the Contractor has _____ days to notify the Board of his new address.

10
21
45
60

_____ days is the maximum time after commencing construction for the contractor to give notice to the owner of his lien rights.

- 30
- 45
- 60
- 90

19. An action for breach of a written contract must be brought within ____ years.

- 2
- 3
- 4
- 5

20. All of the following must follow the OSHA standards except _____ .

A. religious establishments
B. general contractor with one employee
C. landscape contractors
D equipment rental businesses

The type of estimate that provides precise statements of quantities of materials, equipment and manpower is considered to be a(n) _____ .

A. Materials estimate
B. Activity estimate
C. Preliminary estimate
D. Detailed estimate

22. When preparing an equipment estimate, _____ would not need to be evaluated.

A. The drawings
B. All the activity estimates
C. An inspection of the site
D. Safety factors involved

23. Under the completed contract method, the contractor may realize the profit _____ .

A. When the bid is accepted by the owner
B. When the contract is 50% complete
C. When the project is nearly complete
D. When the owner signs off on the final release

A secondary qualifying agent has pulled a permit for a building project. There is a problem with payment to a subcontractor. _____ is responsible for the payment to the subcontractor.

A. primary qualifier
B. both primary & secondary have joint responsibility
C. secondary qualifier
D. owner of the company

In the event of the death of the qualifying agent, _____ may finish an existing project that is under contract with the deceased qualifier.

A. any one
B. secondary qualifier
C. wife of the contractor
D. no one

Please See Answer Key on following page

1 Exam Prep
2017 Contractors Manual
Questions and Answers – 1

		Page
1.	B	7-32
2.	A	6-5
3.	C	4-14
4.	B	10-64
5.	C	10-63
6.	B	10-63
7.	B	8-7
8.	D	8-6
9.	A	9-11
10.	D	9-21
11.	B	3-78, 10-34
12.	B	10-67
13.	A	10-63
14.	B	3-80
15.	C	6-98
16.	A	9-104
17.	C	2-22
18.	B	9-21
19.	D	8-23
20.	A	7-7
21.	D	10-12
22.	D	10-13
23.	C	3-80
24.	A	2-21
25.	A	2-89

1 Exam Prep
2017 Contractors Manual
Questions and Answers – 2

1. A citation issued by a code enforcement officer shall include all of the following, except:

A. A brief description of the violation
B. The name of the code enforcement officer
C. The procedure for the person to follow in order to pay the penalty or contest the violation
D. The name of the person who filed the complaint

2. The type of contract that is best from the owner's perspective is where there is the least variation in the contract price. This type of contract is known as a _____.

A. time & material contract
B. lump sum contract
C. unit price contract
D. cost-plus contract

3. Which of the following is a non-recordable work related injury according to OSHA?

A. cutting away dead skin
B. tetanus shot
C. treatment of infection
D. butterfly dressing in lieu of sutures

For a labor (manpower) estimate, there are various factors which affect production and would include all of the following, except:

A. size of the crew
B. skill & experience of crafts workers
C. supervision available on site
D. site accessibility

5. The type of insurance that covers the contractor for losses of material in transit to the job site is known as _____.

A. Liability insurance
B. Builders Risk
C. Auto liability
D. Fidelity bond

A general contractor may do which of the following according to the license law requirements on a residential project?

A. construct a main sewer collection system
B. install clay tiles on a roof
C. install all mechanical equipment
D. place all pool lines and equipment at the pool

7. Drug free work place programs are generally implemented by an employer to help improve their safety record. If an employer wishes -to institute a drug free work place program he must provide <u>days n</u>otice to all existing employees prior to beginning any testing.

- 0
- 60
- 45
- 30

8. According to the Contractors Manual, if at all possible, keep sling angles greater than _____ degrees.

- 25
- 45
- 60
- 90

An employee is paid a gross weekly amount of $900.00 for the first week of the year. For FUTA tax, how much will the total payment be? Assume no state tax credit

- $45.42
- $54.00
- $55.80
- $108.00

10. If a subcontractor is officially terminated from a contract, his equipment and materials should remain on the site until _____ .

A. the date of official termination
B. the date of letter of notice from the owner
C. until the subcontractor's work is complete
D. until the project is complete

11. In CSI-MASTERFORMAT, Specifications are typically divided into _____ specific divisions to provide a standard reference.

A. 10
B. 50
C. 36
D. 12

12. Long lead items needed for a project should be _____ .

A. purchased prior to bid date
B. handled as a substitution
C. identified & ordered early
D. included on material checklist

Employee Linda was paid a gross total wage of $63,500 last year. What was the total amount withheld from her pay for Medicare and Social Security? (choose closest answer)

$4,295
$4,403
$4,858
$5,002

14. A cost-plus contract can best be described as a contract that is_____.

A. negotiated & open ended
B. fixed sum contract
C. stipulated maximum price
D. based on unit bid prices

15. Which of the following is a concern of the Fair Labor Standards Act? (FLSA)

A. Age discrimination
B. Child labor
C. Vacation time
D. Job safety

16. Which of the following is *not* a method of scheduling within the Network Analysis Technique.

RSM
CPM
PERT
CPA

17. What type of contract encourages cost savings and value engineering?

A. guaranteed maximum price
B. lump sum
   cost plus-fee
   fixed price

18. Of the following, whose lien will be paid first?

Architect
General Contractor
Supplier of a Supplier
Laborer

19. Which of the following oral contacts is enforceable?

A. a job for $400 to last eighteen months
B. a job for $475 to last 180 days
C. a job for $512 to last 14 days
D. oral contracts are not enforceable

20. A procedure is which progress billings are accelerated by assigning higher values to contract portions to be completed in the early stages of a contract is known as _____ .

A. accelerated billings
B. bid rigging
C. bid balancing
D. front end loading

21. The Florida Department of Environmental Protection be notified _____ working days in advance of a demolition for a project where no asbestos is present.

A. 10
B. 5
C. 21
D. does not apply

22. The maximum allowable civil penalty that can be imposed by OSHA for each willful or repeated violation is _____ .

$70,000
$124,471
$125,000
$131,118

Which of the following would have jurisdiction over dredging or excavation of navigable waters and wetlands?

A. U.S. Dept. of the Interior
B. Florida Dept. of State
C. Florida Dept. of Transportation
D. U.S Army Corps of Engineers

24. In the event the qualifying agent resigns from the employment of a contractor, the contractor must replace the qualifier within _____ days.

120
90
60
30

25. When employing a nonresident alien, which of the following taxes must be paid?

A. Medicare and Social Security
B. Income Tax
　FUTA
　all of the above

1 Exam Prep
2017 Contractors Manual
Questions and Answers – 2

1.	D	2-92
2.	B	3-78, 10-34
3.	B	Page 7-23 – 7-25
4.	C	10-30
5.	B	4-7
6.	A	2-78
7.	B	6-98 12.(b)
8.	B	7-90
9.	B	3-182
10.	C	10-69
11.	B	10-7
12.	C	10-24
13.	C	3-171
14.	A	10-34
15.	B	5-11
16.	A	10-57
17.	A	10-35
18.	D	9-81
19.	B	8-6
20.	D	10-74 – 10-75
21.	A	10-97
22.	B	7-31
23.	D	1-16
24.	C	2-20
25.	D	3-184

1 Exam Prep
2017 Contractors Manual
Questions and Answers - 3

Which construction site requires a licensed contractor for the job?

    state university
    federal courthouse
    bank
    post office

How long is the company required to retain OSHA 300/300A logs?

    3 years
    4 years
    5 years
    7 years

An unfair labor practice charge must be received by the regional office with jurisdiction over the area where this alleged unfair labor practice occurred. What is the time limit to file this charge?

    6 months
    1 year
    1-1/2 years
    3 years

A contractor must serve a copy of the claim of lien on the owner and lender (if any) within how many days of the date the claim of lien is recorded?

    15
    30
    60
    90

Which of the following must be true for a person to qualify for a state certification of competency?

    be a resident of the state of Florida
    be a minimum on 21 years of age
    be of good moral character and submit a financial statement
    be of good moral character, be at least 18 years of age and pass an examination

What type of insurance must all certified contractors carry and maintain to work in the state of Florida?

- fire, builder's risk, worker's compensation
- public liability and property damage in the amounts as set by the board
- liability, property damage and completed operations in the amounts as set by the board
- auto, independent contractor's liability, completed operations

According to the Federal unemployment Tax Act, if a contractor acquires a business from someone else who was an employer liable for FUTA tax, you _____.

- may count the wages that employer paid to the employees who continue to work for you when you figure the wage limit
- must pay a tax rate based on the premise that you are a new employer with new employees
- you may pay taxes based on percentage of days in balance of fiscal year
- may count the wages that employer paid to up to three employees who continue to work for you when you figure the wage limit

Automobile insurance rates are filed based on which factors?

- different size vehicles, distance of travel, various uses of the vehicles
- age and condition of vehicles, distance of travel, various uses of the vehicles
- different size vehicles, condition of vehicles, various uses of the vehicles
- various uses of the vehicles, different size vehicles, age of vehicles

A proposed short term project schedule should be reviewed by all the following except _____.

- in-house staff
- subcontractors
- critical material vendors
- building department officials

Florida's right-to-work laws prohibit:

- Union Shop Agreements
- Agency Shop Agreements
- Maintenance of Membership Agreements
- all of the above

Which of the following statements concerning surety bonding is true?

- losses are not contemplated in surety bonds
- surety bonding is a two party agreement
- surety bonding uses the principal of indemnity to spread the losses among policy holders
- surety bonding uses the law of large numbers to determine premiums

Which of the following would require a license/certification/registration number?

    pencils with the company name used as advertising
    vehicles with the company name on the outside
    business stationary
    articles of clothing with the company name

The project schedule of a construction contract will state that the work is to begin at which of the following specific times?

    the permit issuance date
    a particular calendar date
    the notice of commencement of the work
    a start date often described by a milestone

Claims arising from damages that resulted from a contractor's work that already has been finished would be covered by a _____.

    completion bond
    commercial general liability policy
    builder's risk insurance policy
    manufacturer's and contractor's liability policy

Insurance premiums on Worker's Compensation are based on employer's classification code, and per _____ of payroll.

    $1.00
    $50.00
    $100.00
    $1,000.00

According to the Statute of Limitations in the Contractors Manual, how long does a person have to bring action on a wage recovery claim?

    2 years
    5 years
    7 years
    10 years

According to Contractors Manual, "categories on the income statement" include all the following except _____.

    revenues
    expenses
    inventory
    income

What is a disadvantage of a network analysis?

    it is a tedious and exacting task if attempted manually
    it prevents any deviation from the scheduling being noticed quickly
    it prohibits splitting up the project into activities
    it prevents determining the shortest length of time for completion

Registration form SS-4 "Application for Employer Identification Number" must be filed (when applicable) on or before the _____.

    7th day after the date on which business begins
    14th day after the date on which business begins
    30th day after the date on which business begins
    60th day after the date on which business begins

Which of the following is an advantage of a regular corporation?

    limited taxation
    reduced record keeping
    tax deductible fringe benefits
    closely regulated

According to Contractors Manual, if a construction company's federal employment taxes for the quarter ending September 30th have been paid on time, the IRS Form 941 for the quarter ending September 30th must be filed not later than _____.

    October 10th
    October 31st
    November 10th
    November 30th

Premiums for builders risk insurance are based upon _____.

    gross revenue from a project
    net profit from a project
    value of the work in place
    type of work used on the job

What is the maximum fine for failure to provide appropriate notice to the Division of Workers' Compensation for each injury/accident?

    $100
    $250
    $500
    $1,000

Under Florida law, the beneficiaries of a worker killed in a covered workplace accident are entitled to _____.

    a $10,000 death benefit and $7,500 in funeral costs
    up to $150,000 in death benefits and up to $7,500 in funeral costs
    two thirds the employee's wages for life with 5% annual cost of living increase
    two thirds the employee's wages for 104 weeks plus up to $7,500 in funeral costs

What is the difference between salaried workers and hourly wage earners?

    salaried workers are paid for all overtime
    salaried workers always have a higher hourly rate of pay
    salaried workers never have time cards that reflect a specific job
    salaried workers receive the same base amount every pay period

What type of insurance is issued to protect the contractor for loss of **EARNINGS** as a result of damage to or destruction of buildings or equipment?

    Business Interruption
    Business Floater
    General Liability
    Contractor Protective Liability

Within how many days after the subcontractor or supplier began work or furnished materials on the job must a Notice to Owner be given to the owner?

    15 days
    30 days
    45 days
    60 days

Which of the following is a numbered listing of the financial categories shown in the general ledger?

    chart of accounts
    income statement
    check register
    purchase order journal

Which method of accounting will result in the quickest revenue recognition?

    the completed contract method
    the partial contract method
    the percentage of completion method
    the percentage of billings to date method

According to the *Veteran's Re-employment Laws,* military leave of absence must be granted to any permanent full time or permanent part-time employee who enlists or is drafted into active duty in the armed forces. Discharging an employee without cause, who has been rehired and is covered under the law, is prohibited for a period of _____ if the employee's military service period was less than 180 days and more than 30 days.

    6 months
    1 year
    1 year and 6 months
    2 years

The *Employment and Training of Veterans Act* applies to government contractors and subcontractors with contracts worth at least _____.

    $10,000
    $15,000
    $75,000
    $100,000

The *Employee Polygraph Protection Act* prohibits employers from requiring employees or job applicants from taking a lie detector test unless the testing of an employee is _____.

    in connection with the consumption of alcohol on the job site
    in connection with the use of drugs or alcohol at the work place
    in connection with an ongoing investigation involving economic loss to the employer's business
    in connection with the misappropriation of funds by the employee

Which of the following items is not included as part of General Conditions?

    substitutions
    workmanship and materials
    bid bond
    shop drawings

Under the "completed contract" method of revenue recognition, which one the following determines if the project is complete enough to recognize profit?

    the final inspection date has been set
    billings totaling in excess of 98% to 99% of contract value been approved
    the architect has issued a Certificate of Payment of Substantial Completion
    the lending institution has rolled the construction loan into a permanent loan

According to Contractors Manual, a lawsuit to enforce an oral contract must be brought within_____

    2 years
    3 years
    4 years
    5 years

If a contractor wants to insure construction materials completely, from the time the materials leave the place of shipment until the materials reach their destination and are installed, the contractor should purchase a(an) _____.

    motor truck cargo owner's policy
    transportation policy
    contractor's equipment floater
    installation floater

According to Contractors Manual, which party has lien rights?

    sub-sub-subcontractor
    laborer for sub-subcontractor
    material supplier providing materials sold just for stock and not for direct delivery to the site
    material man providing materials to another material man

As a prerequisite to initial licensure or renewal of a license as certified or registered contractor, general and building contractors must carry which of the following minimum insurance amounts?

    $100,000 liability/$25,000 property damage
    $250,000 liability/$75,000 property damage
    $300,000 liability/$50,000 property damage
    $500,000 liability/$100,000 property damage

The Lien Laws require that any person who receives funds for constructing or altering improvement, use the funds to pay others for services and materials provided in connection with the project.

person who does **not** comply with this requirement may be _____.

A. subject to discipline under the Contractor Licensing Laws only
B. criminally prosecuted under the Lien Law for a misdemeanor and subjected to discipline under the Contractor Licensing Law
C. criminally prosecuted under the Lien Law for a misdemeanor only
D. criminally prosecuted under the Lien Law for felony and subjected to discipline under the Contractor Licensing Law

According to the Florida Statues, Chapter 489, a contractor was found guilty of allowing their certificate to be used by uncertified persons with intent to evade the provisions of Chapter 489. The Construction Industry Licensing Board may revoke the certificate of the contractor, require financial restitution to a consumer, and impose an administrative maximum fine of _____.

    $5,000
    $5,000 or assess costs associated with investigation and prosecution
    $10,000
    $10,000 or assess costs associated with investigation and prosecution

Which is a possible penalty for knowingly making false statements, representations, or certifications in any application, record, report, plan or other document filed as part of the OSHA requirements?

    loss of license and 90 days in prison
    maximum fine of $5,000 or one year in prison, or both
    a maximum fine of $10,000 or 6 months in prison, or both
    maximum fine of $20,000 and loss of license

A joint venture is a profit-seeking combination of two or more parties that _____.

    are registered with the Secretary of State for a specific purpose
    are limited to construction of a project that does not exceed the equity deposits of all partners
    must have at least one licensed partner
    are generally limited to a specific project or undertaking

A qualifying agent for a business organization _____.

    must requalify the business the business every two years
    is qualified to act for the business in all matters connected with contracting
    has the obligation to notify the governor when his address changes
    keeps the company president from having to visit the job sites

A contractor is filing Form 941 for taxes which were withheld from employees for the first quarter of the year (January, February, and March). All the taxes were deposited when they were due. According to Contractors Manual, what is the LATEST date (without penalty) that the contractor can file this return?

    April 15
    April 30
    May 10
    May 15

When does *Form W-4* (Employee's Withholding allowance Certificate) expire?

    January 31
    February 15
    when the employee gives the employer a new *Form W-4*
    February 16

According to the Florida Construction Lien Law, one way an owner can minimize duties under the Construction Lien Law is for the owner to _____.

    require that the contractor obtain a payment bond
    post an irrevocable letter of credit
    record a notice of commencement
    require the contractor to provide him with a release of lien

The ratio that is determined by adding cash, accounts receivable and marketable securities together and dividing by current liabilities is referred to as the _____.

    current ratio
    quick ratio
    leverage ratio
    debt to equity ratio

The two most commonly used *liquidity* ratios are the _____.

    liquidity ratio and the leverage ratio
    activity ratio and the quick ratio
    current ratio and the quick ratio
    liquidity ratio and the profitability ratio

A contractor enters into a written contract with a supplier for $10,000 worth of materials. The contractor then agrees orally to pay the supplier $15,000 for the materials if they can be delivered ahead of schedule. The supplier delivers the materials ahead of schedule and the contractor refuses to pay more than $10,000. The agreement for $15,000 is _____

    unenforceable because the Statute of Frauds requires all contracts for goods in excess of $500 to be in writing.
    unenforceable because the Statute of Frauds requires all contracts for personal services to be in writing.
    C. enforceable because it is an oral modification of an existing contract made between contracting parties.
    D. enforceable because the Statute of Frauds does not require sales of goods between merchants to be confirmed.

Which of the following do not have lien rights?

    materialman supplying materials to a subcontractor
    materialman supplying materials to a sub-subcontractor
    engineer with a direct contract with owner
    materialman supplying materials to another material man

Please see answer key on the following page

1 Exam Prep
2017 Contractors Manual
Questions and Answers – 3

1. C 2-6
   A bank is not government property and requires a licensed contractor for the job.

2. C 7-16

3. A 5-14

4. A 9-30

5. D 2-76, §489.111

6. B 2-19

7. A 3-182

8. A 4-12

9. D 10-64

10. D 5-14

11. A 4-13

12. B Ch. 2, §489.119 (5)(c) & (d)

13. D 8-13

14. B 4-10 – 4-11

15. C 6-15

16. A 8-23

17. C 3-30

18. A 10-58

19. A 1-20

20. C 1-13

21. C 3-156

22. C 4-11

C6-12

B6-161

D3-49

A4-8

C9-21

A3-25

C3-79

B5-45

D5-46

C5-50

C10-10

B3-80

C8-23

D4-7

B9-18

C2-157

D9-120, §713.345(b) note all are felonies

D2-95, §489.129(1)

C7-17

D1-12

B1-20, 2-20

C3-156

C3-168

46.   A   9-46

B3-89

C3-89

A8-6 – 8-7

D9-18

1 Exam Prep
2017 Contractors Manual
Questions and Answers - 4

A qualifying agent for a business entity, who was in charge of a construction project undertaken by that business entity, is disciplined by the Construction Industry Licensing Board for willful or deliberate disregard and violation of applicable building codes. According to Florida Construction Industry Licensing Law, if any officer, director, or member of the business entity knew or should have known of the violation and failed to take corrective action, the Board may impose a maximum combined total administrative fine, per violation, against the business entity and the qualifying agent of _____.

- $ 2,500
- $ 5,000
- $ 7,500
- $10,000

A "secondary" qualifying agent is responsible for _____.

- the company's financial matters only on jobs where the agent's license was used to obtain the permit
- supervision of field work at sites where the agent's license was used to obtain the permit
- items designated by the primary qualifying agent of the company
- all qualifying matters as qualifying agent when the original qualifier leaves the company

Real estate may be depreciated using _____.

- a straight line method
- an adjusted basis method
- any accelerated method
- the double declining balance method

When can a Notice of Commencement be extended past one year?

- if it is written into the Notice of Commencement
- if the job proceeds past one year
- when there is an architectural change order
- never

Which is NOT a delay factor when determining production efficiency percentages?

- accessibility of site
- financial incentives
- poorly trained personnel
- weather conditions

According to Fair Labor Standards Act, which will eliminate the contractor's liability for paying overtime pay?

- an agreement that only 8 hours per day or 40 hours per week will be counted as working time
- an outside salesperson who works on straight commission and qualifies as exempt
- an announcement by an employer that overtime work will only be paid for if authorized in advance
- an announcement by an employer that no overtime work will be permitted

According to Florida Contractors Manual, which is an advantage of leasing?

- lower overall cash flows than purchasing
- reduced front-end cash outlays
- generates depreciation for tax purposes
- cheaper than owning in the long run

A secondary qualifier is never responsible for _____.

- safety at the jobsite
- permits they pulled
- the quality of work at the jobsite
- financial matters

All chains, being used as a sling, should be inspected once a _____ by a competent inspector.

- day
- week
- month
- year

Which of the following is NOT a prohibited agreement under Florida's Right to Work Law?

- union shop agreements
- agency shop agreements
- federal enclaves agreements
- maintenance of membership agreements

Failure of a certificate holder or registrant to apply for renewal of an active certificate at the time of biennial renewal shall cause the certificate to become _____.

- temporarily suspended
- permanently suspended
- voluntarily inactive
- delinquent

Claims arising from damages that resulted from a contractor's work that already has been finished would be covered by a _____.

    completion bond
    completed operations liability policy
    builder's risk insurance policy
    manufacturer's and contractor's liability policy

What is the purpose of the Lien Law payment bond?

    to exempt the contractor from construction liens
    to exempt the subcontractor from construction liens
    to protect the owner's property from construction liens
    to allow easy payments to subcontractors

Under the Civil Rights Act of 1964 (Title VII), the maximum compensatory and punitive damages a plaintiff may recover from an employer of 95 people is _____.

    $24,000
    $50,000
    $100,000
    $250,000

According to National Council on Compensation Insurance, a contractor's worker's compensation premiums can be reduced by any of the following, except _____.

    participating in a co-insurance program
    joining an insurance pool
    participating in a deductible program
    requiring the employee to pay part of the premium

Under the Florida Human Rights Act of 1992, (Chapter 760, FL. Statue) back pay liability is limited to _____ months prior to filing of complaint.

    6
    18
    24
    36

An employer with 40 employees is cited by OSHA for a high severity, greater probability violation. The employer has had one other citation in the last 3 years. Using ONLY the information given, what would be the proposed penalty for this violation?

    $5,000
    $8,730
    $10,907
    $11,224

How long after the subcontractor's final furnishing of labor, services, or material for a job does the subcontractor have for recording a valid Claim of Lien?

    45 days
    60 days
    90 days
    one year

The quarterly Federal Tax Form 941 summarizes tax liability for the employer and includes _____

    liability insurance
    federal income taxes withheld
    workers compensation insurance
    federal unemployment insurance tax

A properly registered fictitious name is valid for _____.

    1 year
    2 years
    3 years
    5 years

Which type of bond is a guarantee to the owner that the project will be completed according to the terms and conditions specified in the contract?

    payment bond
    bid bond
    performance bond
    completion bond

According to the Internal Revenue Service, employers must keep all employment tax records for at least how many years?

    2 years
    4 years
    5 years
    7 years

For purposes of unemployment compensation, misconduct connected with work does not include _____.

    A. wrongful intent or evil design
    B. deliberate disregard of employee duties
    C. deliberate disregard of behavior standards
    D. isolated instances of negligence and poor judgment

Which of the following companies would be required to have Worker's Compensation Insurance?

- a company that is not in the construction business that leases 2 employees
- a company in the construction business that hires employees
- a corporation in the construction business with 2 employees who are both officers of the corporation and have certificates of election to be exempt
- a corporation that is not in the construction business with 2 employees who are both officers of the corporation and have certificates of election to be exempt

A Notice to Owner from a non-privity lienor must be sent within _____ days after the first furnishing of labor or materials.

- 30
- 45
- 72
- 90

A construction company that is not tax exempt has received a materials only bid from the supplier in the amount of $3,500. Who is responsible for the collection and reporting of the state sales tax when the material is purchased?

- the supplier
- the owner of the building
- the construction company only
- no one; no sales tax is required

When progress billings bring in more income than costs incurred during the early stages of a contract, the contractor is using _____.

- a draw system
- a pre-qualified payment method
- front end loading
- the critical path method

When preparing a bid, the contractor notes that the specifications require one type of equipment, but the plans show a different type. The contractor should _____.

- bid based on using the least expensive of the two
- follow the plans
- follow the specifications
- substitute comparable equipment

What is required to file a construction claim of lien?

- permission from the owner
- a court order
- a direct contract with the owner
- the claim must be recorded with the clerk of the court

Which is a requirement for an employee to recover under a compulsory State Workers' Compensation Statute?

- the injury must occur while the employee is engaged in interstate commerce
- the injury must arise out of and in the course of employment
- the injury must arise out of the negligence of the employer or fellow employee
- the injured employee must be a permanent full-time employee

The Drug-Free Workplace Act of 1988 _____.

- does not require drug testing
- always applies to subcontractors
- applies to contractors in foreign countries
- applies only to contractors with more than 50 workers

Which of the following can be added to a Builder's Risk policy by means of an extended coverage endorsement?

- vandalism coverage
- malpractice coverage
- materials in transit
- catastrophic flood coverage

Which bond requires a low bidding contractor who fails to enter into a contract to pay a penalty equal to the amount of the bid?

- performance bond
- forfeiture obligation
- difference in bid
- payment

The Statute of limitations requires that an action for breach of an unwritten contract must be brought within a maximum of _____.

- 2 years
- 4 years
- 5 years
- 7 years

Which of the following wages would not be subject to Federal Unemployment tax paid by the employer?

    wages paid to a Canadian who frequently enters the U.S. to work as a carpenter
    severance pay
    wages paid to a deceased worker's estate in the same calendar year as the date of the worker's death
    D. wages paid to the employer's spouse

A contractor required to carry Worker's Compensation insurance may fulfill the requirements of the law by _____.

    obtaining liability insurance at three times the coverage generally required
    seeking individual self-insured status through the Department of Labor and Employment Security
    C. obtaining major medical insurance for all employees
    D. obtaining life insurance policies for all employees

How many employees must a contractor have for the Florida Workers' Compensation Act to be applicable?

    1
    2
    3
    4

A certified contractor operating as the qualifying agent and sole owner of a corporation was the low bidder on a project. The contractor died after the bid was awarded but before the work started. The executor of the contractor's estate is not a licensed contractor. Can the project legally be started by the deceased contractor's firm and administer by the executor?

    yes, but only if the executor obtains a registered or certified qualifying agent within 30 days of the death of the contractor
    yes, but only if the executor employs a registered or certified contractor as superintendent
    yes, but only if the board approves it
    no

OSHA regulations require that injury and illness records be retained in each establishment for _____ calendar year(s) following the end of the year to which they relate.

    1
    3
    5
    7

Which activity is one of the most commonly followed preliminary project planning steps?

    develop milestone check point list
    obtain and review plans and specifications
    relate project days to calendar days
    scheduling the project

Which of the following statements is true?

    you must file a claim of lien within 45 days of the last day you furnish labor and supply materials
    if the contract is less than $1,500 and you are not in privity with the owner, you may still have lien rights
    claim of lien must be served on the owner before or within 45 days after it is recorded
    if claim of lien of lien is from a non-privity lienor (sub-subcontractor), Notice to Owner must be served on both the owner and the contractor

When estimating the cost of transporting equipment to the job site, the estimator should use _____

    the actual speed limits
    the average of the speed limits
    30 to 40% of the speed limits
    40 to 65% of the speed limits

Accounts receivable are classified as _____.

    assets
    credits
    debits
    liabilities

A construction company that is not tax exempt has received a materials only bid from the supplier in the amount of $3,500. Who is responsible for the collection and reporting of the state sales tax when the material is purchased?

    the supplier
    the owner of the building
    the construction company only
    no one; no sales tax is required

A recorded Notice of Commencement will expire in 90 days unless _____.

    Notice to Owners are filed
    work has commenced
    first payment to contractor is released
    first inspection is made

When making a claim of lien, you must send a sworn statement of account within _____.

    90 days after demand of statement has been made
    30 days after demand of statement has been made
    45 days before demand of statement has been made
    15 days before demand of statement has been made

What are two types of manpower estimates?

    comparative and historical
    graphic and detailed
    preliminary and detailed
    preliminary and historical

Which of the following is NOT insurance?

    Surety Bonding
    Contractors Equipment Floater
    Transportation Policy
    Inland Marine Insurance

According to Florida Unemployment Compensation Laws, an employer who fails to file reports when due will be assessed a penalty of _____ per report for each month (or fraction thereof) that the report is delinquent.

    $25
    $50
    $75
    $100

According to Florida Contractors Manual, who has the responsibility to initiate safety programs?

    only general contractor
    employer
    project engineer
    safety engineer

Please see answer key on the following page

1 Exam Prep
2017 Contractors Manual
Questions and Answers – 4

    D2-95, §489.129(1)

    B2-21, 2-89, §489.1195 (2)(e)

3.   A   3-34

    A9-88, §713.13 (1)(a)7.(c)

5.   B   10-30

6.   B   5-15

7.   B   3-93

8.   D   2-89, §489.1195 (2)(e)

9.   C   7-89

10.   C   5-14

11.   D   2-84, §489.116 (4)

12.   B   4-9

13.   C   4-14, 9-46

14.   B   5-35

15.   D   6-26

16.   C   5-36

17.   B   7-32
    (high severity, greater probability = base penalty of $12,471)

    Ch. 7
    (adjustment factor = -30% for 26 to 100 workers)

    Note: there is no 10% reduction for good past history because there was one other violation in the last 3 years

Solution: $12,471 x .70 (100% - 30%) = $8,730 proposed penalty

C9-84

B3-177, 3-179

D1-15

C4-14

B3-154

D5-302

B6-5

B9-76

A3-63

C3-108, 10-74

C10-6

D9-84, §713.08 (5)

B6-26

A5-49

C4-7

B4-13

B8-23

D3-184

B6-9

A6-5

C2-89, §489.121

C7-16

B10-58

D9-75, §713.06 (2)(a)

D10-27

A3-16

A3-63

B9-12

B9-98, §713.16 (2)

C10-28

A4-13

A5-53

B7-36

1 Exam Prep
2017 Contractors Manual
Section 61G4 – Practice Test

The term advertise does not refer to which of the following?

    articles of clothing
    business cards
    contracts
    signs on vehicles

Which of the following may not verify a roofing contractor's active experience?

    General Contractor
    Residential Contractor
    Specialty Contractor
    Building Contractor

The proper aggregate amount of insurance for a General Contractor is $_____ of Liability and $_____ of Property.

    $50,000, $25,000
    $100,000, $25,000
    $150,000, $50,000
    $300,000, 50,000

4. A business organization which loses its qualifying person shall have _____ days from the date the qualifier terminated his affiliation within which to obtain another qualifying person.

    7
    14
    30
    60

5. A claim against the Recovery Fund must be made within _____ after the conclusion of any civil, criminal, administrative action or award in arbitration based on the act.

    30 days
    60 days
    1 year
    2 years

6. "Classroom Hour" means _____ of instruction, inclusive of any breaks, recesses, or other time not spent in construction.

    A. 45 minutes
    B. 50 minutes
    C. 60 minutes
    D. 65 minutes

All registered contractors and certified contractors are required to complete _____ hours of continuing education each renewal each renewal cycle.

    14
    16
    21
    24

8. If a contractor makes a false statement of insurance coverage, and this is his third offense, the minimum punishment is _____.

    A. $2,500 fine
    B. $2,500 fine and probation or suspension
    C. $5,000 fine
    D. $5,000 fine and probation or suspension

9. For the purpose of certification, a passing grade shall be valid only for a period of _____ from the date the list of successful candidates is approved by the board.

    A. 60 days
    B. 1 year
    C. 2 years
    D. 4 years

10. The application and examination fee for an applicant for certification shall be _____.

    $290
    $300
    $335
    $350

1 Exam Prep
2017 Contractors Manual
Section 61G4 – Answers

A. 61G4-12.011(3) –2017 Contractors Manual, pg 2-149

C. 61G4-15.001(a)–2017 Contractors Manual, pg 2-153

D. 61G4-15.003(h) –2017 Contractors Manual, pg 2-157

D. 61G4-15.009 –2017 Contractors Manual, pg 2-160

C. 61G4-21.003(5) –2017 Contractors Manual, pg 2-202

B. 61G4-18.002(3)–2017 Contractors Manual, pg 2-192

A. 61G4-18.001(1)–2017 Contractors Manual, pg 2-190

D 61G4-17.001 –2017 Contractors Manual, pg. 2-186 - 2-187

D 61G4-16.005 –2017 Contractors Manual, pg 2-182

C 61G4-12.009(1)(a) –2017 Contractors Manual, pg 2-147

1 Exam Prep
2016 Circular E
Questions and Answers

An employer shall keep for at least _____ years all records of employment taxes.

    1
    2
    3
    4

How many banking (business) days does a semi-weekly depositor have to deposit withholding taxes?

    1
    at most 2
    at least 3
    at least 4

If a contractor deducted less than the correct amount of tax from any wage payment, the contractor _____.

    A. is required by law to inform the employee in writing within five working days B. may deduct the amount of under collection from later payments to the employee
    C. must fill out form 988B and return it to the internal revenue service within 12 working days D. must make up the difference from the contractor's own funds within 10 workingdays

If, at the end of a quarter, a contractor's total FUTA tax is $150, the contractor _____.

    may add the tax to the amount for deposit for the next quarter
    must deposit the tax during the first month after the quarter
    must deposit the tax during the second month after the quarter
    must deposit the tax during the third month after the quarter

A contractor employs a full time college student in his construction business paying him gross wages of $500 per week. The contractor is required to pay/report which federal taxes if this student is in a work-study program established by his college?

    none
    Income tax (only)
    Income tax & FICA (only)
    Income tax & Federal Unemployment tax (only)

An employer is liable for the unemployment tax, if in the current or preceding calendar year_____

- The employer paid at least $500 in wages in a calendar quarter
- The employer paid at least $1,000 in wages in a calendar quarter
- The employer had at least one employee for any portion of a day in 10 different calendar weeks in a year.
- The employer had at least one employee for any portion of a day in 20 different weeks in a year

For federal tax purposes, which of the following is not considered an employee?

- Agent/Driver delivering food
- Real Estate agent
- Traveling sales selling hotel supplies for one company
- Part-time worker

If an employer withholds income tax from an employee's regular wages, the employer may withhold a flat for supplemental wages.

- 5%
- 10%
- 20%
- 25%

When taxes are not deposited when due and the delay is more than 16 days late, a penalty is charged.

- 5%
- 10%
- 15%
- 20%

Deposits for FUTA taxes are due by .

- The 15th day of the month following the end of the quarter
- By the 5th day of the next month following the quarter
- By the last day of the first month after the quarter ends
- At the end of the eighth monthly period

11. The maximum credit against the FUTA for payments to state unemployment funds is .

- 2.8%
- 3.5%
- 5.4%
- 6.2%

12. An employee's gross pay in the first pay period of the year is $675. The employee is single, has 2 withholding allowances, and is paid bi-weekly. The amount of the employee's income tax withholding is _____.
(Select closet answer).

    $32
    $27
    $40
    $57

For FUTA tax purposes, an employer is any person or organization that has paid wages of _____ or more in any calendar quarter.

    $500
    $1,000
    $1,500
    $2,000

A household employee in a private home, age 20, is paid $100 a week salary and has worked 25 weeks. Which taxes are required?

    Income Taxes and FICA
    FICA and Federal unemployment taxes
    Federal unemployment taxes and income taxes
    None of the above

15. You must use _____ to make all federal tax deposits.

    EFT
    FICA
    Form 940
    WBC

16. Given: An employee's gross *weekly* payroll for a certain week is shown below. Use the *Percentage Method* to determine the withholding.

Marital Status	Total # Exemptions	Hourly Wage	Regular Hours	Overtime Hours
Married	3	$21.00	35	0

The total amount of Federal Income Tax (only), to be deducted from the gross wages is _____. (choose closest answer)

    $34
    $40
    $44
    $52

17. As of Dec. 31, 2015, an employer has 3 employees; each will be paid a salary as shown below:

Employee #1 — $70,000
Employee #2 — $52,000
Employee #3 — $49,500

The total amount of FICA taxes that the employer will have to deposit will be _____.

$15,484
$25,995
$12,998
$26,239

According to the Federal unemployment Tax Act, if a contractor acquires a business from someone else who was an employer liable for FUTA tax, you _____.

may be able to count the wages that employer paid to the employees who continue to work for you when you figure the $7,000 FUTA tax wage base.
must pay a tax rate based on the premise that you are a new employer with new employees
you may pay taxes based on percentage of days in balance of fiscal year
may count the wages that employer paid to up to three employees who continue to work for you when you figure the wage limit

The quarterly Federal Tax Form 941 summarizes tax liability for the employer and includes _____

liability insurance
withheld income taxes and/or FICA
workers compensation insurance
federal unemployment insurance tax

Which of the following wages would not be subject to Federal Unemployment tax paid by the employer?

wages paid to a Canadian who frequently enters the U.S. to work as a carpenter
severance pay
wages paid to a deceased worker's estate in the same calendar year as the date of the worker's death
wages paid to the employer's spouse

According to Circular E instructions, if filing electronically, Copy A of all Forms W-2 shall be sent to the Social Security Administration (SSA) by _____.

January 31
February 16
February 28
March 31

A contractor is filing Form 941 for taxes which were withheld from employees for the first quarter of the year (January, February, and March). All the taxes were deposited when they were due. What is the LATEST date (without penalty) that the contractor can file this return?

    April 15
    April 30
    May 10
    May 15

When does *Form W-4* (Employee's Withholding allowance Certificate) expire?

    January 31
    February 15
    Only if the employee has a life change *(for example, if marital status changes)*
    December 31

Tom is single, is paid $420 per week, and claims 1 allowance. Using the bracket method, how much should be withheld for income tax each paycheck?

    $52
    $49
    $41
    $37

If you are paid with a car instead of money, _____ is used to determine the value of the car for tax purposes

    purchase price
    fair market value
    blue book
    manufacturers' standard retail price

1 Exam Prep
Answers - 2016 Circular E

Note: all pages below are the pages within 2016 Circular E, not the Florida Contractors Manual page numbers

1)	D	pg. 6,	Recordkeeping
2)	C	pg. 26	Deposits on Business Days Only
3)	B	pg. 33	Collecting underwithheld taxes from employees
4)	A	pg. 35	Depositing FUTA Tax
5)	C	pg. 40	Chart
6)	D	pg. 34	General Test
7)	B	pg. 11	Who Are Employees?
8)	D	pg. 18	Supplemental Wages
9)	B	pg. 28	Deposit Penalties
10)	C	pg. 35	When to Deposit FUTA Taxes
11)	C	pg. 34	Computing FUTA Tax
12)	B	pg. 50	Wage Bracket Method Tables
13)	C	pg. 34	Who Must Pay?
14)	B	pg. 38	Chart
15)	A	pg. 24	How To Deposit
16).	A	pgs. 42-44	Married paid weekly, Table 1(b) on page 3-192. Employee earns $735 for the week. ($21 x 35 = $735) Then deduct allowances. (3 x 77.90 = $233.70) $735 - $233.70 = $501.30. Use the first line in Table 1(b). "$0.00 plus 10% of excess over $164" $501.30 - $164 = $337.30; 10% is $33.70. A. is closest.
17)	D	pg. 23	Social Security and Medicare Taxes ($70,000 + 52,000 + 49,500) x 7.65% x 2 = $26,239.50
18)	A	pg. 35	Successor Employer
19)	B	pg. 29	Filing Form 941 or Form 944
20).	D	pgs. 36	Chart
21)	D	pg. 8	By March 31
22)	C	pg. 8	By April 30… (but read explanation changing to May 10)
23)	C	pg. 20	Effective date of Form W-4
24)	D	pg. 46	Wage Bracket Method
25)	B	pg. 15	Wages not paid in money

1 Exam Prep
Business and Finance – State
FLSA – 15 Questions
The following questions are from the 2017 Florida Contractors Manual

At _____ years of age, youth may be employed unlimited hours in any occupation other than one declared to be hazardous by the Secretary of Labor.

- 16
- 17
- 18
- 21

A secretary is hired on a salary basis of $425 per week for a work schedule of Monday through Friday 8:00 am to 3:00 pm with 1/2 hour lunch daily. In week #2 she works 45 hours. Her gross pay for week #2 is _____.

- $498.00
- $559.70
- $598.98
- $621.30

The "regular rate" must be calculated for:

- Any hourly employee working less than 40 hrs / week
- Exempt employees
- Non-exempt salaried employees working over 40 hrs / week
- Administrative personnel

4. According to FLSA, the minimum wage pay may be not less than _____ per hour.

- $8.00
- $5.15
- $3.25
- $7.25

5. Regardless of the pay period, the act _____ allow the averaging of hours over 2 or more weeks to arrive at a single work week hourly figure.

- sometimes
- does not
- does
- None of the above

Which of the following is most likely exempt from overtime provisions?

- Laborer on salary
- Laborer on hourly wage
- Office messenger on salary

D. Office manager

Overtime pay should be paid at not less than _____ times the regular hourly wage after 40 hours in one work week.

    A. .5
    1.5
    1.75
    2 (if work falls on a holiday or weekend)

If an employee earns $10 per hour for a 50 hour week. How much is the overtime compensation?

    $100
    $50
    $150
    $550

A non-exempt employee earns a salary of $450/week on a fluctuating work week and works 50 hours in a particular week, what is her gross pay?

    $398
    $415
    $481
    $495

Employers are required by regulation to keep so called "hard records" such as payroll, employment contracts, sales and purchase records for their employees a minimum of _____.

    2 years
    3 years
    4 years
    5 years

According to Fair Labor Standards Act, which will eliminate the contractor's liability for paying overtime pay?

    An agreement that only 8 hours per day or 40 hours per week will be counted as working time.
    An outside salesperson who works on straight commission and qualifies as exempt.
    An announcement by an employer that overtime work will only be paid for if authorized in advance.
    An announcement by an employer that no overtime work will be permitted

Which of the following is not in accordance with requirements for an executive being granted an exemption from the Fair Labor Standards Act?

    primary duty of managing a company subdivision
    regularly directs 3 to 4 employees
    receives a salary of $150 per week
    regularly exercises discretionary power

Given: A contractor hires a day laborer at a rate of $45.00 for one day's work. The contractor uses the laborer for six days in one work week. The laborer average 8-1/2 hours of work per day. The laborer is entitled to _____ .

    A. A gross pay of less than $400.00 for the six days of work.
    B. A gross pay between $400.00 and $450.00 for the six days of work.
    C. A gross pay between $451.00 and $500.00 for the six days of work.
    D. A gross pay of over $500.00 for the six days of work

FLSA regulations do not address _____ .

    vacation
    holiday pay
    severance payments
    all of the above

John makes flags at the factory. He makes 8 flags per hour. He is paid $1.00 per flag, and last week, he made 350 flags. What is John's gross pay from last week?

    $320.00
    $350.00
    $365.00
    $380.00

1 Exam Prep
Business and Finance - FLSA Answers
The following answers are from the 2017 Florida Contractors Manual

1. A   Pg. 5-157   Florida Contractors Manual (FCM)

2. D   Pgs. 5-21 & 5-22   FCM
   $425 ÷ 32.5 hours usually worked = $13,08/hour regular rate
   $13.08 x 1.5 = $19.62 OT rate
   $13.08 x 40 = $523.20; $19.62 x 5 = $98.10; 523.20 + $98.10 = 621.30

3. C   Ch. 7   FCM

4. D   Ch. 5   FCM

5. B   Ch. 5   FCM

6. D   Ch. 5   FCM

7. B   Ch. 5   FCM

8. C   Ch. 5   FCM

9. D   Pg. 5-24   **Fixed Salary for Fluctuating Hours,** FCM
   $450 ÷ 50 = $9.00 (regular rate)
   $9.00 x 50 = $450 (fluctuating hours regular pay)
   $9.00 x .5 = $4.50 (rate for the 10 OT hours)
   $4.50 x 10 = $45.00 (pay for OT to be added to the Regular & OT pay)
   $450.00 + $45.00 = $495.00 Total Gross Pay

10. B   Pg. 5-30   **Hard Records,** FCM

11. B   Ch. 5   FCM

12. C   Ch. 5   FCM

13. B   Ch. 5   FCM
    $45 ÷ 8 hours = $5.63 per hour, but minimum wage is $7.25//hour
    Hours for week are 8.5 x 6 = 51; 40 at regular rate, 11 at OT rate
    OT rate is $10.88 ($7.25 x 1.5)
    40 x $7.25 = $290; 11 x $10.88 = $119.68;
    $290.00 + $119.68 = $409.68

14. D   Ch. 5   FCM

15. C. Pg. 5-22   **Piece Worker**, FCM

First, did John make 350 flags in 40 hours? o 8 flags per hour can be made.
- o   8 x 40 = 320
- o   So, there are still 30 flags to be considered. He HAD to work overtime to make them. Let's come back to that.

In the 40 hours it took to make the 320 flags, what is John's <u>base hourly rate</u>?
He is paid $1.00 per flag, makes 8 flags per hour, so base rate is $8.00/hour.
So, for the first 40 hours, he made $320.00: 40 x $8.00 =

$320.00 For the other 30 flags, how long did John have to work?

He makes 8 flags per hour; so 30 ÷ 8 = 3.75.
3.75 hours is the amount of overtime he worked to make the extra 30 flags.

Overtime is calculated at 1.5 times base rate, also known as 'time and a half'.
So, to get overtime rate: 1.5 x $8.00 = $12.00

John worked 3.75 hours of overtime at $12.00 per hour: 3.75 x $12.00 = $45.00

To calculate last week's pay: $ 320.00 Regular/Base Pay
                                <u>$ 45.00 Overtime Pay</u>

                                $ 365.00 Total Gross Pay

1 Exam Prep
2017 Contractors Manual
Unemployment Compensation Practice Test

If an individual is found to be eligible to draw unemployment compensation and his average weekly wage for the base period is $173.30, his weekly benefit would be _____.

- $74.00
- $78.00
- $82.00
- $86.00

Unemployment benefit payments will not be charged to the account of the employer under which of the following conditions?

- Individual left his job without good cause
- Individual was discharged for misconduct
- Individual refused without good cause an offer of suitable employment
- All of the above

If an individual is found to be eligible to draw unemployment compensation and his average weekly wage for the base period is $164.50, his weekly benefit amount would be _____.

- $76.00
- $80.00
- $81.00
- $82.00

Unemployment contributions by employers shall become due at which of the following times?

- Immediately following the quarter for which they are payable
- Two weeks after the dose of the calendar quarter for which they are payable
- Within 15 days after the close of the calendar quarter for which they are payable
- Shall be paid on or before the last day of the month following the close of the calendar quarter for which they are due.

Each employer shall post and maintain printed statements concerning benefits and rights relative to the administration of Chapter 443 FS in which of the following places?

- The front door of his office
- His private office
- A conspicuous place
- In places readily accessible to individuals in his employment

The worker must wait _____, for which no benefits are payable, after filing an initial claim.

    1 day
    3 days
    1 week
    2 weeks

The unemployed worker's average weekly pay is $18.00. He is entitled to _____ unemployment compensation per week.

    $0
    $9.00
    $18.00
    $20.00

The Unemployment Compensation law states you are an "employer" if, during each of twenty different calendar weeks during a given calendar year _____.

    Ten or more employees were employed
    3 or more employees were employed
    4 or more employees were employed
    1 or more employees were employed

If an individual is found to be eligible to draw unemployment compensation and his average weekly wage for the base period is $224.60, what would his weekly benefit amount be?

    $94.00
    $95.00
    $125.00
    $112.00

If an individual is found to be eligible to draw unemployment compensation and his average weekly wage for the base period is $500.00, his weekly benefit amount would be _____.

    $200.00
    $225.00
    $250.00
    $500.00

An employer who is delinquent by 60 days in filing the required unemployment compensation reports shall be assessed a penalty of _____ unless the division finds that such employing unit has or had good reason for failure to file such report or reports.

    5%
    10%
    $50.00
    $100.00

According to the Unemployment Compensation law, you are an employer if _____.

    The most you paid in employee wages in any quarter is $400.00
    You had some person employed for one (1) day in 15 different calendar quarters
    You buy a business which was classified as an employer at the time of acquisition
    All of the above

In addition to meeting regular benefit requirements, a worker whose unemployment is due to a labor dispute _____.

    Is automatically ineligible
    Is automatically ineligible as long as the dispute exists
    Is eligible to collect benefits if the unemployment results from a "lockout" by the employer.
    Is ineligible for a period of seven weeks; then becomes eligible

An employer knowingly making a false statement or report in connection with administration of the unemployment compensation laws can be fined up to _____ and/or imprisoned for up to ____ years.

    $2,500.00, 2
    $5,000.00, 5
    $5,000.00, 10
    $7,500.00, 5

You are required to keep work records for unemployment tax auditing for at least _____ years.

    3 years
    4 years
    5 years
    6 years

1 Exam Prep
2017 Contractors Manual
Unemployment Compensation Answers

Question	Answer	Page
1.	D	5-53
2.	D	5-53
3.	D	5-53
4.	D	5-52
5.	C	5-53
6.	C	5-52
7.	A	5-53
8.	D	5-52
9.	D	5-53
10.	C	5-53
11.	C	5-53
12.	C	5-52
13.	C	5-52
14.	B	5-53
15.	C	5-53

1 Exam Prep
Florida State Lien Law
Questions and Answers

Which of the following is a lienable item?

    Post office
    V.A. Hospital
    County courthouse
    Leased car rental ticket counter in an airport

If a "SUMMONS TO SHOW CAUSE" is served upon a lienor, the lien of any lienor upon whom such notice is served and who fails to institute a suit to enforce his or her lien within _____, shall have their lien extinguished automatically.

    15 days
    60 days
    45 days
    20 days

Which of the following is the correct priority of payment for liens claimed under a direct contract?

    Liens of the contractor, liens of all persons other than the contractor, liens of all laborers.
    Liens of the contractor, liens of all laborers, liens of all persons other than the contractor.
    Liens of all persons other than the contractor, liens of all laborers, liens of the contractor.
    Liens of all laborer, liens of all persons other than the contractor, liens of the contractor.

Which of the following have lien rights?

Laborer working for a supplier, supplying a sub contractor
Material suppliers to a sub-subcontractor
Sub-subcontractors
Material supplier to a material supplier, supplying to the general contractor

    1,2, and 3
    2,3, and 4
    1,3, and 4
    1,2, and 4

One way an owner can minimize the risk of having a lien filed on his or her property is to _____.

- have the contractor submit an affidavit that all persons are paid
- stay active on the project and talk to the subcontractors
- have the contractor obtain a performance bond
- have the contractor obtain a payment bond

A claim of lien may be recorded at any time during the progress of the work or thereafter but not later than _____ days after the final furnishing of the labor, services, or materials by the lienor.

- 30
- 45
- 60
- 90

The only method of extending a lien beyond the one year deadline is if _____.

- an action is filed in court to enforce the lien.
- an extension of lien is requested.
- the lien is re-recorded.
- a notice of lien has been sent to the owner.

A notice to owner must be served by a subcontractor before commencing, or not later than _____ days after commencing furnishing services or materials.

- 30
- 45
- 60
- 90

A lienor, who is a privity lienor, is one _____.

- whose lien has been filed
- whose lien has been satisfied
- with direct contract with the owner
- with a contract with other than the owner

A contractor must serve a copy of the claim of lien on the owner and lender (if any) within how many days of the date the claim of lien is recorded?

- 15
- 30
- 60
- 90

If the direct contract is greater than _____, the applicant shall file with the issuing authority prior to the first inspection either a certified copy of the recorded notice of commencement or a notarized statement that the notice of commencement has been filed.

    $1,000
    $2,500
    $3,500
    $5,000

According to Contractors Manual, which party has lien rights?

    sub-sub-subcontractor
    laborer for sub-subcontractor
    material supplier providing materials sold just for stock and not for direct delivery to the site
    material man providing materials to another material man

The Lien Laws requires that any person who receives funds for constructing or altering improvement, use the funds to pay others for services and materials provided in connection with the project.

person who does **not** comply with this requirement may be _____.

A. subject to discipline under the Contractor Licensing Laws only
B. criminally prosecuted under the Lien Law for a misdemeanor and subjected to discipline under the Contractor Licensing Law
C. criminally prosecuted under the Lien Law for a misdemeanor only
D. criminally prosecuted under the Lien Law for felony and subjected to discipline under the Contractor Licensing Law

Which of the following do not have lien rights?

    materialman supplying materials to a subcontractor
    materialman supplying materials to a sub-subcontractor
    engineer with a direct contract with owner
    materialman supplying materials to another material man

According to Florida Construction Lien Laws, which of the following is considered an improper payment by an owner to a contractor?

    a payment made before notice of commencement expires
    before any notice to owner is received
    after a notice to owner has been served and a waiver of release has been obtained by the owner
    payments made by owner after a notice to owner has been served and before a waiver has been obtained by the owner

When may a person who has delivered materials that were unused for an improvement peaceably repossess and remove such materials?

- Upon written demand
- When the improvement is completed
- When the improvement is abandoned
- Both B and C are correct

How long does a clam of lien last?

- 1 year
- 3 years
- 5 years
- 7 years

What is required to file a construction claim of lien?

- permission from the owner
- a court order
- a direct contract with the owner
- the claim must be recorded with the clerk of the court

An owner may terminate Notice of Commencement by executing a Notice of Termination that contains all except which of the following?

- recording office document book and Page reference numbers and date of Notice of Commencement
- two copies of a Notice Direct Contract
- statement that lienors have been paid in full
- statement specifying that notice applies to all real property subject to Notice of Commencement

If an owner makes payment to a contractor, without requiring a final payment affadavit (a/k/a contractor's affadavit) the payments are considered _____.

- improper payments
- refused payments
- unrecoverable payments
- non-essential payments

The Lien Laws requires that any person who receives funds for constructing or altering improvement, use the funds to pay others for services and materials provided in connection with the project.

A person who does **not** comply with this requirement may be _____.

A. subject to discipline under the Contractor Licensing Laws only
B. criminally prosecuted under the Lien Law for a misdemeanor and subjected to automatic suspension under the Contractor Licensing Law
C. criminally prosecuted under the Lien Law for a misdemeanor only
D. criminally prosecuted under the Lien Law for felony

All of the following are part of the amount necessary to transfer a lien to a bond or cash except:

100% of the lien amount
$25 filing fee
Interest at the legal rate for three years
The greater of $1,000 or 25% of the lien amount for costs and attorney fees

A notice of lien filing or a Notice to Owner shall be given to the Owner via _____.

hand delivery in person
certified return receipt U.S. mail
posting on the job site
all of the above

A recorded Notice of Commencement will expire in 90 days unless _____.

Notice to Owners are filed
work has commenced
first payment to contractor is released
first inspection is made

If an owner fails to file a Notice of Commencement on a project with a total cost of $10,000, the contractor will initially be unable to obtain _____.

approval of Building Inspections
Certificate of Completion
final payment from the owner
final Certificate of Occupancy

1 Exam Prep
Florida State Lien Law
Answers

1.	D	Ch. 9, §713.02	Florida Contractors Manual
2.	D	Page 9-31, §713.21(4)	Florida Contractors Manual
3.	D	Ch. 9 §713.06(4)(a)	Florida Contractors Manual
4.	A	Page 9-61	Florida Contractors Manual
5.	D	Ch. 9 §713.02(6)	Florida Contractors Manual
6.	D	Ch. 9 §713.08(5)	Florida Contractors Manual
7.	A	Ch. 9 §713.22)	Florida Contractors Manual
8.	B	Ch. 9 §713.06(2)(a)	Florida Contractors Manual
9.	C	Page 9-21 or 9-67, §713.05	Florida Contractors Manual
10.	A	Page 9-30	Florida Contractors Manual
11.	B	Page 9-92, §713.135	Florida Contractors Manual
12.	B	Page 9-17	Florida Contractors Manual
13.	D	Page 9-41 & 9-91, §713.345(1)(d)	Florida Contractors Manual,
14.	D	Page 9-17 and 9-66, §713.03	Florida Contractors Manual
15.	D	Page 9-20 or 9-68, §713.06 (2)(a)	Florida Contractors Manual
16.	D	Page 9-96, §713.15	Florida Contractors Manual
17.	A	Page 9-30	Florida Contractors Manual
18.	D	Ch. 9, §713.08(5)	Florida Contractors Manual
19.	B	Ch. 9, §713.132(1)	Florida Contractors Manual
20.	A	Page 9-38	Florida Contractors Manual
21.	D	Ch. 9, §713.345(1)(d)	Florida Contractors Manual
22.	B	Page 9-45	Florida Contractors Manual
23.	D	Ch. 9, §713.06(2)(a)	Florida Contractors Manual
24.	B	Ch. 9, §713.18	Florida Contractors Manual
25.	A	Ch. 9, §713.135(d)	Florida Contractors Manual

1 Exam Prep
State Business and Finance
Workers' Compensation

In reference to Worker's Compensation, if anyone knowingly conceals payroll, makes a misleading statement, or otherwise causes damages of $150,000, the offender commits _____.

   a first degree misdemeanor
   a third degree felony
   a second degree felony
   a first degree felony

The workers compensation program provides payment for part of the wages an employee might lose if the job related injury or illness disables the employee for more than ___ days.

   3
   7
   14
   21

The maximum death benefit that workers compensation will pay is _____.

   $10,000
   $50,000
   $150,000
   D, $250,000

Payments made by the Florida Workers' Compensation Insurance for a temporary total disability are based on the rate of _____ of the employee's average weekly wage object to a maximum of $700.

   50%
   66 2/3%
   75%
   85%

Construction industry employers who have _____ or more employees are required to have workers compensation insurance.

   10
   3
   2
   1

Any employer or insurance carrier who fails or refuses to send any report required of him by the workers compensation law shall be subject to a civil penalty not to exceed _____ for each failure or refusal.

    $100
    $500
    $1,000
    $5,000

An employee who suffers an employment related injury shall inform his/her employer within ____ day(s) of the injury

    30
    15
    3
    1

In most cases, if an employee receives disability and workers compensation payments at the same time, both payments together cannot be more than _____ of what the employee was earning before injury.

    50%
    60%
    70%
    80%

Any agreement by an employee to contribute to a benefit fund to provide medical services as required by Workers' Compensation _____.

    is Invalid
    is not in violation of Workers' Compensation
    is a misdemeanor
    is valid as long as one registers the agreement with the department of insurance

If an employee is injured, the employer must file a report of injury with the insurance carrier and the division of workers' compensation within _____ days of learning of the injury.

    3
    5
    7
    10

In Florida, Worker's Compensation will pay up to _____ for funeral costs.

- $1,000
- $7,500
- $10,000
- $15,000

The Division of Worker's Compensation does not consider _____ to be a construction business.

- remodeling existing structures
- clearing land for construction purposes
- rebuilding existing structures
- well drilling on land with existing buildings

A contractor's employee injured her leg on the job on March 15, causing a loss of 18 work days. What is the latest date that the employee may report the accident to the employer in order to be covered under Workers' Compensation?

- March 22nd
- March 30th
- April 14th
- April 29th

In order to file for an exemption to Worker's Compensation, the applicant must own ____ of the company.

- 5%
- 10%
- 20%
- 33%

According to the Florida Worker's Compensation Law, first aid cases requiring treatment on site that do not require medical treatment for which charges will be incurred, and do not disable the employee for more than _____, do not need to be reported.

- 3 hours
- 1 day
- 3 days
- 7 days

Insurance premiums on Worker's Compensation are based on employer's classification code, and per _____ of payroll.

- $1.00
- $50.00
- $100.00
- $1,000.00

According to the Workers' Compensation law, the term "person" means .

- An individual
- A partnership
- A corporation
- All of the above

No compensation shall be payable if an injury was caused primarily by _____.

- Intoxication of the employee.
- The employee being under the influence of a narcotic.
- By the willful intention of the employee to the injure or kill himself
- All of the above.

Which of the following companies would be required to have Worker's Compensation Insurance?

- a company that is not in the construction business that leases 2 employees
- a company in the construction business that hires employees
- a corporation in the construction business with 2 employees who are both officers of the corporation and have certificates of election to be exempt
- a corporation that is not in the construction business with 2 employees who are both officers of the corporation and have certificates of election to be exempt

Which is a requirement for an employee to recover under a compulsory State Workers' Compensation Statute?

- the injury must occur while the employee is engaged in interstate commerce
- the injury must arise out of and in the course of employment
- the injury must arise out of the negligence of the employer or fellow employee
- the injured employee must be a permanent full-time employee

A contractor required to carry Worker's Compensation insurance may fulfill the requirements of the law by _____.

   obtaining liability insurance at three times the coverage generally required
   seeking individual self-insured status through the Department of Labor and Employment Security
C. obtaining major medical insurance for all employees
D. obtaining life insurance policies for all employees

Which activity is considered to be a construction job, as that term is used in the Worker's Compensation Stature?

   roof replacement
   a homeowner's building of their own premises
   well drilling on land containing existing structures
   manufacturing of materials used in construction work

When an injury is caused by the refusal of an employee to use a safety device or to observe a safety rule or statute, then _____.

   no compensation shall be paid
   compensation may be reduced by 10%
   compensation may be reduced by 25%
   compensation may be reduced by 50%

If a judge of compensation claims determines that an injured employee at the time of an accident is a minor, in violation of the child labor laws of Florida, the employer shall, in addition to the normal compensation and death benefits… pay such additional compensation as the judge of compensation claims may determine … however the total compensation shall not exceed _____.

   $100,000
   $250,000
   double the amount otherwise payable
   triple the amount otherwise payable

An Employer not having a drug-testing program shall ensure that at least _____ elapse between a one-time notice to all employees that a drug-testing program is being implemented and the beginning of actual drug testing.

   ten days
   thirty days
   forty-five days
   sixty days

1 Exam Prep
Answers - State Business and Finance
Workers' Compensation

Answer		Chapter	Section
1)	D	Ch. 6	440.105(4)(f)3.
2)	B	Ch. 6	440.12(1)
3)	C	Ch. 6	440.16(1)(b)
4)	B	Ch. 6	440.15(2)(a)
5)	D	Ch. 6	440.02(17)(b)(2)
6)	B	Ch. 6	440.185(8)
7)	A	Ch. 6	440.185(1)
8)	D	Ch. 6	440.15(9)
9)	A	Ch. 6	440.21
10)	C	Ch. 6	440.185(2)
11)	B	Ch. 6	440.16(1)(a)
12)	D	Ch. 6	page 6-6
13)	C	Ch. 6	440.185(1)

The employee has 30 days to report the injury. Injury was on March 15th.
March = 31 days - 15 days = 16 days remaining, + 14 days (30 days) into April = April 14th

14)	B	Ch.6	page 6-43
15)	D	Ch. 6	page 6-12
16)	C	Ch. 6	page 6-15
17)	D	Ch. 6	440.02(23)
18)	D	Ch. 6	440.09(3)
19)	B	Ch. 6	6-5, 6-23
20)	B	Ch. 6	6-26
21)	B	Ch. 6	6-9
22)	A	Ch. 6	6-6
23)	C	Ch. 6	440.09(5)
24)	C	Ch. 6	440.54
25)	D	Ch. 6	440.102(3)(a)(12)(b)

1 Exam Prep
2017 Contractors Manual
Ch. 7 - Rope, Wire, & Chains Questions

According to the Florida Contractors Manual, for general rigging, the Safety Factor is ____ for materials.

    2
    3
    5
    10

A contractor needs to determine the safe working load of a ¾" nylon rope. There are no manufacturers' charts or tables for the contractor to refer to. The mathematical safe working load (SWL) calculation would yield a SWL of _____ lbs.

    2,160
    4,000
    960
    540

Wire rope with a tensile strength of 224,000 - 246,000 PSI is referred to as _____.

    grade 110/200, improved plow steel
    grade 120/130 extra improved plow steel
    grade 100/110, plow steel
    mild plow steel

The safe working load (SWL) for a rope with a breaking strength of 2000 lbs. is _____ lbs., if the rope is being used to hoist materials.

    2,000
    400
    200
    1,000

If at all possible, keep sling angles greater than _____.

    360°
    180°
    90°
    45°

The single most important rigging precaution is determining _____ before attempting to lift them.

> the type of loads
> the weight of the loads
> the SWLs of the rope
> the distribution of the loads

When manufacturer's charts are not available, SWL can be calculated by dividing the _____ by the _____.

> breaking strength, factor of safety
> weight of the load, factor of safety
> factor of safety, weight of the load
> breaking strength, weight of the load

What is the SWL of 7/8" nylon rope?

> 1,820 lbs.
> 2,080 lbs.
> 2,940 lbs.
> 3,270 lbs

What is the SWL of 3/8" nylon rope?

> 360 lbs.
> 410 lbs.
> 490 lbs.
> 540 lbs.

What is the SWL of 3/8" polyethylene rope?

> 315 lbs.
> 340 lbs.
> 440 lbs.
> 505 lbs.

What is the SWL of 1/2" nylon rope?

> 360 lbs
> 386 lbs
> 620 lbs
> 960 lbs

Which of the following manila rope grades is the standard hoisting rope, and usually has an identifying trademark?

    Yacht rope
    Number 1 grade
    Bolt rope
    Number 2 grade

Which of the following is not one of the most commonly used rope splices?

    short splice
    Flemish eye splice
    sailor splice
    long splice

Fiber ropes are made from _____.

    natural fibers only
    synthetic fibers only
    both natural and synthetic fibers
    animal hair

Which of the following is true?

    Safe Working Load = Breaking Strength ÷ Factor of Safety
    Safe Working Load = Breaking Strength + Factor of Safety
    Breaking Strength - Factor of Safety = Safe Working Load
    Safe Working Load + Breaking Strength = Factor of Safety

According to the Florida Contractors Manual, for general rigging, the Safety Factor is ____ for personnel.

    5
    8
    10
    12

For safe rope use, _____.

    avoid all but straight line pulls
    never use natural fiber rope
    inspect ropes once a year
    all of the above are true

In general, all running ropes (except elevator ropes) in continuous service must be inspected _____.

- twice a day, at the beginning and end of service
- once every working day
- at the end of each work week
- once a month

The breaking test of 7/8" dacron rope at 25.0 lbs. per 100 feet is _____ lbs.

- 11,500
- 10,400
- 20,050
- 18,000

The maximum working load of 7/8" dacron rope at 25.0 lbs. per 100 feet is _____ lbs.

- 1,252
- 1,980
- 2,070
- 3,200

1 Exam Prep
2017 Contractors Manual
Ch. 7 - Rope, Wire, & Chains - Answers

1.   C   7-53   Contractors Manual

2.   A   7-56   Contractors Manual
   3/4 = 6/8, 6 x 6 x 60 = 2160

3.   C   7-67   Contractors Manual

4.   B   7-53   Contractors Manual
   2000 ÷ 5 = 400 (Material SWLs require a division of 5)

5.   D   7-90   Contractors Manual

6.   B   7-65   Contractors Manual

7.   A   7-53   Contractors Manual

8.   C   7-56   Contractors Manual
   Square the numerator, multiply by 60. 7 x 7 = 49. 49 x 60 = 2,940 lbs.
   Note that '60' above, is the multiplier for Nylon, per chart on pg. 7-56

9.   D   7-56   Contractors Manual
   Square the numerator and multiply by 60. 3 x 3 = 9. 9 x 60 = 540 lbs.
   Note that '60' above, is the multiplier for Nylon, per chart on pg. 7-56

10.   A   7-56   Contractors Manual
    Square the numerator and multiply by 35. 3 x 3 = 9. 9 x 35 = 540 lbs.
    Note that '35' above, is the multiplier for Polyethylene, per chart

11.   D   7-56   Contractors Manual
    First the numerator of 1/2 must be converted to eighths. ½ = 4/8
    To change to eighths from 1/2, you first make the denominator (2) into the denominator 8. So, 2 x 4 = 8. Then we must also multiply the numerator by 4.
    1 x 4 = 4.
    Square the numerator and multiply by 60. 4 x 4 = 16; 16 x 60 = 960 lbs.
    Note that '60' above, is the multiplier for Nylon, per chart on pg. 7-56

12.   B   7-50   Contractors Manual

13.   C   7-59   Contractors Manual

14.   C   7-50   Contractors Manual

15.	A	7-53	Contractors Manual
16.	C	7-53	Contractors Manual
17.	A	7-57	Contractors Manual
18.	B	7-75	Contractors Manual
19.	D	7-54	Contractors Manual
20.	B	7-54	Contractors Manual Per chart: maximum working load is 11% of Breaking Test; Breaking Test = 18,000 lbs; 18,000 x .11 (11%) = 1,980 lbs.

1 Exam Prep
Florida Chapter 455: Business and Professional Regulations
Questions and Answers

The provision that any CILB licensee who is a member of the Armed Forces of the United States on active duty shall be kept in good standing without registering paying dues or completing CE is found in _____?

    455.02
    455.212
    455.201
    455.11

A qualified individual seeks professional licensure as a residential contractor and is not a United States citizen, which section of FS 455 addresses his qualifications to practice?

    455.2125
    455.10
    455.11
    455.02

The $5.00 fee imposed upon initial licensure and subsequent renewals is used _____.

    to cover administrative costs
    to offset inflation and increased salaries
    to combat unlicensed activity
    as a fee to help fund investigative background checks

An inactive status licensee may change to active status at any time, provided the licensee _____.

    pays all fees due and takes an additional 6 hours of continuing education
    meets all requirements for active status, pays any additional license fees due necessary to equal those imposed on an active status licensee, pays any applicable reactivation fees, and meets all continuing education requirements.
    meets all requirements for active status, pays any additional license fees due necessary to equal those imposed on an active status licensee, pays a penalty reactivation fee of $70, and meets all continuing education requirements
    A and C are both correct

Which of the following would qualify as grounds for disciplinary action?

    Failing to report to the department any person the licensee knows is in violation of this chapter
    Practicing or offering to practice beyond the scope permitted by law
    Using a Class III or a Class IV labor device without having registered such a device
    All of the above

The Board shall meet at least once _____.

   Monthly
   Quarterly
   Twice each calendar year
   Annually

Unlicensed practice of a profession is punishable by an administrative penalty not to exceed _____.

   $500
   $1,000
   $5,000
   $12,500

Failure of a licensee to renew before a license expires shall cause the license to become _____.

   delinquent
   inactive
   void
   inactive until payment of a late fee and completion an additional 4 hours of continuing education

The Board shall forward all fingerprints to _____.

   the Dept. of State and the Dept. of Law Enforcement
   the Dept. of Law Enforcement and the Federal Bureau of Investigation
   the Dept. of State and the IRS
   the Dept. of Alcohol Tobacco and Firearms and the Dept. of Law Enforcement

The penalty for theft or reproduction of an examination constitutes _____.

   a misdemeanor
   a felony of the first degree
   a felony of the second degree
   a felony of the third degree

1 Exam Prep
Florida Chapter 455: Business and Professional Regulations
Answers

1. A   455.02
2. C   455.11
3. C   455.2281
4. B   455.271(4)
   - D   455.227
   - D   455.207(3)
   - C   455.228(1)
   - A   455.271(5)
   - B   455.213(10)
   - D   455.2175

1 Exam Prep
Construction Industry Licensing Board
Florida Chapter 489

Which of the following applies to a qualifying agent of corporation?

- He is only qualified to act for the business during normal working hours
- He is qualified to act for the corporation in all matters connected with its construction business
- He does have authority to supervise in all areas of the company's business
- None of the above

A contractor who loans his license may be fined up to _____.

- $1,000
- $2,000
- $3,000
- $5,000

If a contractor is disciplined by the board and is the qualifying agent for a business organization and the violation was performed in connection with a construction project undertaken by that business organization, the board may impose an additional administrative fine not to exceed _____ against the business organization or against any partner, officer, director, trustee, or member if such person participated in the violation or knew or should have known of the violation and failed to take corrective action.

- $500
- $1,000
- $2,500
- $5,000

A person who is registered or holds a valid certificate from the board may go on voluntary inactive status on payment of a renewal fee during the inactive period, not to exceed _____ per renewal period.

- $10
- $50
- $30
- $40

With respect to an applicant for a certificate, the initial certification fee and the renewal fee shall not exceed _____.

- $350
- $100
- $150
- $250

An active certified residential contractor is eligible to take the general contactors' examination if he possesses a minimum of years of proven experience in the classification in which he is certified.

- 1
- 2
- 3
- 4

The services of a building contractor are limited to commercial and residential buildings which do not exceed stories in height.

- 1 1/2
- 2
- 2 1/2
- 3

The board, by rule, may establish delinquency fees for late renewal not to exceed ____ for certification.

- $40
- $20
- $30
- $50

If an incomplete contract exists at the time of death of a contractor, the contract may be completed by any person, though not certified or registered, with the board's approval. That person must notify the board within ____ days after the death of the contractor, of his/her name and address.

- 15 days
- 30 days
- 45 days
- 60 days

In a contracting company that has more than one qualifying agent, a secondary qualifying agent is responsible for _____.

- the supervision of field work at sites where his license was used to obtain building permits
- the supervision of field work at sites where the secondary qualifying agent acts in a supervisory manner
- the financial matters for projects that used his license to obtain building permits
- the financial matters for projects where the secondary qualifying agent acts in a supervisory manner

Which of the following must be true for a person to qualify for a state certification of competency?

- be a resident of the state of Florida
- be a minimum on 21 years of age
- be of good moral character and submit a financial statement
- be of good moral character, be at least 18 years of age and pass an examination

Which of the following is not exempt from Chapter 489?

- Contractors who work on bridges and roads
- An employee of a licensed contractor working within the scope of that license
- Inspector of a nuclear power plant
- An authorized employee of the United States or Florida

According to the Florida Statues, Chapter 489, a contractor was found guilty of allowing their certificate to be used by uncertified persons with intent to evade the provisions of Chapter 489. The Construction Industry Licensing Board may revoke the certificate of the contractor, require financial restitution to a consumer, and impose an administrative maximum fine of _____.

- $5,000
- $5,000 or assess costs associated with investigation and prosecution
- $10,000
- $10,000 or assess costs associated with investigation and prosecution

A qualifying agent for a business organization _____.

- must requalify the business every two years
- is legally qualified to act for the business in all matters connected with contracting
- has the obligation to notify the governor when his address changes
- keeps the company president from having to visit the job sites

A qualifying agent for a business entity, who was in charge of a construction project undertaken by that business entity, is disciplined by the Construction Industry Licensing Board for willful or deliberate disregard and violation of applicable building codes. According to Florida Construction Industry Licensing Law, if any officer, director, or member of the business entity knew or should have known of the violation and failed to take corrective action, the Board may impose a maximum combined total administrative fine, per violation, against the business entity and the qualifying agent of _____.

- $ 2,500
- $ 5,000
- $10,000
- $15,000

Failure of a certificate holder or registrant to apply for renewal of an active certificate at the time of biennial renewal shall cause the certificate to become _____.

- temporarily suspended
- permanently suspended
- voluntarily inactive
- delinquent

Upon initial signing of an agreement or contract with a home owner, a contractor must deliver a written statement explaining the construction industry recovery fund. This action applies to all repairs, renovations, or construction over _____ in value.

- $500
- $1,500
- $2,500
- $5,000

Your contractor's license number must appear in or on all the following advertisements except_____.

- free yellow Page listings
- coupons
- business proposals
- business cards

A project may be presumed abandoned after ____ days if the contractor terminates the project without just cause.

- 30
- 60
- 90
- None of the above

An active certified air-conditioning Class B contractor is eligible to take the air-conditioning Class contactors' examination if he possesses a minimum of years of proven experience in the classification in which he is certified.

- 1
- 2
- 3
- 4

1 Exam Prep
Construction Industry Licensing Board
Florida Chapter 489
Answers

1)   B   489.119

2)   D   489.129

3)   D   489.129

4)   B   489.109

5)   D   489.109

6)   D   489.111

7)   D   489.105

8)   D   489.109

9)   B   489.121

10)   A   489.1195

11)   D   489.111

12)   C   489.103

13)   D   489.129(1)

14)   B   489.1195(a)

D 489.129(1), plus additional fine per 489.129(2)

D 489.116 (4)

C 489.1425

A 489.119 (5)(a)(b)(c)

C 489.129(j)

A 489.111(2)(c)5.c.

State Flag/Widget Question

John makes widgets at the factory. John makes 8 widgets per hour.
He is paid $1.00 per widget
Last week, he made 350 widgets.

What is John's gross pay from last week?

    $320.00

    $350.00

    $365.00

    $380.00

First, did John make 350 widgets in 40 hours? o
- 8 widgets per hour can be made.
    - o 8 x 40 = 320
    - o So, there are still 30 widgets to be considered. He HAD to work overtime to make them. Let's come back to that.

In the 40 hours it took to make the 320 widgets, what is John's base hourly rate?
He is paid $1.00 per widget, makes 8 widgets per hour, so base rate is $8.00/hour.
So, for the first 40 hours, he made $320.00: 40 x $8.00 = $320.00

For the other 30 widgets, how long did John have to work?
He makes 8 widgets per hour; so 30 ÷ 8 = 3.75.
3.75 hours is the amount of overtime he worked to make the extra 30 widgets.

Overtime is calculated at 1.5 times base rate, also known as 'time and a half'.
So, to get overtime rate: 1.5 x $8.00 = $12.00

We know that John worked 3.75 hours of overtime at $12.00 per hour: 3.75 x $12.00 = $45.00

To calculate last week's pay:
$ 320.00 Regular/Base Pay
$ 45.00 Overtime Pay
$ 365.00 Total Gross Pay

Sample Practice Test
1 Exam Prep
Business and Finance
Simulated Practice Exam for 125 Questions

"Hard Records", such as payroll, employment contracts, sales & purchase records must be retained for _____ years.
- 2
- 3
- 4
- 5

"Soft Records" (time cards, time sheets) must be retained for _____ years.
- 2
- 3
- 4
- 5

FS §489 requires complete financial and business records to be retained for _____ years.
- 2
- 3
- 4
- 5

OSHA logs 300/300A must be retained for _____ years.
- 2
- 3
- 4
- 5

Per the IRS, records of employment taxes must be retained for _____ years.
- 2
- 3
- 4
- 5

Per §455, examination records must be kept _____ years immediately following the examination.
- 2
- 3
- 4
- 5

I-9 forms must be retained _____.
- 3 years from date of hire
- 1 year from date employment ends
- 3 years from date employment ends
- Either A. or B., whichever is longer

Per A.I.A., tests, inspections, and approvals of work shall be paid for by the _____; if tests are failed, additional costs shall be borne by _____.
- Owner, Owner
- Owner, Contractor
- Architect, Contractor
- Contractor, Contractor

The maximum hours of work allowed per week for a 16 year old while school is in session is _____ hours.
- 12
- 18
- 20
- 30

A job has a cost to date of $34,000. The cost to complete is estimated to be $91,000. If the contractor wanted to make a 12% profit, the contract price would be _____.

- $125,000
- $127,400
- $140,000
- $157,340

The _____ regulates the FLSA.

- Department of Labor
- Department of Business and Professional Regulation
- Construction Industry Licensing Board
- Florida Department of State

At least _____ days before the end of a licensure cycle, the department shall forward a licensure renewal notification to an active or inactive licensee at the licensee's last known address of record provided to the department.

- 15
- 30
- 60
- 90

_____ would probably not be subject to the overtime regulations.

- Employees with fluctuating workweeks
- Employees who are employed in the capacity of outside salesman
- Employees who are piece workers
- Employees who are salaried

The Buy American Act does not include _____.

- Mexico
- Canada
- Brazil
- Europe

Per FLSA, an executive employee _____.
- must earn at least $913 per week
- customarily directs the work of 2 or more employees
- has the authority to hire or fire other employees
- all of the above.

An individual who smokes in a non-smoking area is subject to a fine of _____ for a repeat offense.
- $100
- $250
- $500
- $1,000

A _____ would be most likely to receive a Limited License.
- Retired person
- Professional from another state
- Trainee immediately following a natural disaster
- Person who has failed the state test 5 times

_____ is responsible to post OSHA posters on a multi-contractor project?
- The Owner
- The General Contractor
- Each Contractor
- The Project Superintendent

_____, duly authorized agents and employees of DBPR may inspect premises of any establishment at all reasonable hours.
- When there is a suspected OSHA violation
- When there are minors working on the premises
- When the services offered at the premises include authorization to prescribe controlled substances
- When the alcohol is served

A foreign trained, exiled professional may be examined by the department if the professional _____.

    immigrated to the United States from Eastern Europe because of political reasons
    immigrated to the United States from Cuba because of political reasons
    immigrated to the United States from China because of political reasons
    immigrated to the United States from the Western Hemisphere because of political reasons

A maximum of ____ of the required continuing education hours can be fulfilled with the performance of pro bono services.
    10%
    25%
    50%
    75%

The *real turnover ratio* is _____.
    cost of sales over inventory at cost
    cost of sales - retail sales
    retail sales over breakeven point
    overhead plus all costs

In order to obtain a limited license, a person should have been licensed for at least _____ years in any jurisdiction in the United States.
    3
    5
    7
    10

_____ will benefit from those with a limited license.
    Those studying for a license
    Inexperienced business owners
    The indigent
    Retirees

The theft or reproduction of an examination constitutes a _____ .
- Misdemeanor
- Felony of the first degree
- Felony of the second degree
- Felony of the third degree

_____ is a foreseen condition that would not have an effect on Production Efficiency.
- Weather
- Workload
- Deadlines
- Site Area

Florida Diggers bought a tractor for $210,000. It's useful life is 12 years and it has a salvage value of $30,000. If the tractor is sold at the end of year 6, the total depreciation would be _____ .
- $90,000
- $45,000
- $60,000
- $112,000

The Bidder shall deliver the required bonds to the Owner not later than _____ following the date of execution of the Contract.
- 24 hours
- 3 days
- 5 working days
- 7 days

"2% - 10 days, net 30" is _____ .
- an extra charge for shipping
- a discount of 2% if the customer pays the invoice within 10 days
- a discount of 2% if the customer pays the invoice within 30 days
- a discount or a penalty of 2%, depending on the date the invoice is paid

Florida's Right to Work Laws _____.

    prevent discrimination based on race, creed, or color

    allow non-resident aliens with proper documentation the right to work

    prevent employees from being forced to join a union

    all of the above

Under the Florida Worker's Compensation Act, a contractor may recover _____ from a subcontractor who has elected exemption from Chapter 440 if the subcontractor's exemption is invalid and has caused liability to the contractor for an employee of the subcontractor.

    benefits paid and interest due

    a minimum of $1,500 and interest

    penalties up to 100% of their contract

    a maximum of $2,500 per occurrence

According to Florida Contractors Manual, construction project schedules should have progress posted at least _____.

    daily

    weekly

    biweekly

    monthly

A fine of up to _____ can be imposed on a contractor for proceeding on any job without obtaining applicable local building permits.

    $1,000

    $3,000

    $5,000

    $10,000

An OSHA 300 safety log must be maintained by employers with at least ___ employees.

    5

    7

    10

    11

Bidders and Sub-bidders requiring clarification of the Bidding Documents shall make a written request which shall reach the architect at least ____ day(s) prior to the date for receipt of bids.

- 1
- 3
- 5
- 7

According to Florida Contractors Manual, _____ is a correct formula.

- Assets — Liabilities = Equity
- Assets + Liabilities = Owner's Equity
- Assets = Owner's Equity - Depreciation
- Owner's Equity = Liabilities – Depreciation

According to Florida Contractors Manual, the _____ is an estimating method that is *not* recommended for lump sum contracts.

- approximate estimated method
- detailed survey method
- square footage method
- unit price method

The three C's of underwriting that the surety industry considers before a contractor can acquire a bond are _____ .

- character, cash and contracts
- completion percentage, completed contracts and cash
- cash, completion and contracts
- capital, character and capacity

The Florida sales tax is _____ .

- Reported on form DR-15-CS and paid on a monthly basis
- Reported on form DR-15-CS and paid on a quarterly basis
- Reported on form 941 and paid on a monthly basis
- Reported on form 941 and paid on a quarterly basis

Expanding a business usually requires a great deal of capital to purchase new equipment, buildings, or to obtain long term financing. To qualify for expansion financing, financial institutes typically require that you have been in business at least _____, while _____ is preferred.

    A. 2 years; 4 years
    B. 2 years; 5 years
    C. 3 years; 5 years
    D. 3 years; 6 years

If an employer conducts business in more than one location in Florida, completion of Multiple Worksite Report _____ will be required on a quarterly basis.

    FL-13
    UCT-6
    BLS-3020
    P-38

A _____ is a special combination of two or more persons or entities jointly seeking a profit in some specific venture, without an actual partnership or corporate designation

    special limited partnership
    S-type
    joint venture
    sole proprietorship

Fictitious names are valid for ____ years.

    2
    3
    4
    5

Which of the following are prohibited by Florida's Right to Work Laws?

    Union Shop Agreements
    Agency Shop Agreements
    Maintenance of Membership Agreements
    All the above are prohibited

OSHA records must be maintained for _____.

    3 years
    5 years
    6 years
    4 years after the last recordable incident

If the contractor defaults or neglects to carry out the Work, and fails to do so within _____ of receipt of written notice from the Owner, the Owner may correct such deficiencies.

    10 days
    7 business days
    7 calendar days
    3 days

The best way to accurately control petty cash is through a(n) _____.

    imprest system
    separate bank account
    a dedicated entry group within an accounting system
    lock box

OSHA 300, Log on Summary of Occupational Injuries and Illnesses, is used to record _____.

    accident investigations
    all health claims
    all incidents resulting in loss of consciousness
    non-work restricting injuries

ZZZ Construction buys a tractor for $157,500. They are able to depreciate the tractor over seven years. Using the straight line method, the depreciation in the seventh year is _____.

    $10,575
    $22,500
    $16,275
    $33,000

When a contractor has to perform extra work for a subcontractor or material vendor, the contractor will proceed to recover the cost in the form of a(n) _____.

- addendum
- back charge
- change order
- lien

Under the completed contract method, a contract is recognized as complete when it is in excess of _____ complete.

- 75% to 80%
- 90%
- 98% or 99%
- none of the above

A Change Order is a written instrument prepared by the Architect, and signed by _____.

- the owner
- the architect
- the owner and the architect
- the owner, the contractor, and the architect,

Questions 53-55 pertain to the following facts:

Perfect Plus Construction is partway through a job. The cost of work completed is $210,000. It is estimated that completing the job will cost an additional $105,000. The total contract price of the job is $390,000. You have billed, and been paid, $220,000. Using the percentage of completion method, answer the following 3 questions.

What percentage of the job is complete?

- 66.67%
- 60%
- 75.5%
- less than 50%

How much money has been earned on this job?

- $129,870
- $255,719
- $260,013
- $215,303

Which of the following is true?

- You have unearned income.
- You have earned more than you've been paid.
- You have earned exactly what you were paid.
- You have earned less than you have been paid.

The federal minimum wage is _____ per hour.

- $5.15
- $7.25
- $10.75
- $12.35

The job responsibilities of a Superintendent includes _____.

- actively participate in creation of a project schedule
- maintain change order log
- back charge control
- process payroll

Within 3 business days of the date the Contractor becomes aware of an impending or actual cancellation or expiration of any insurance, the Contractor shall provide notice to the _____ .

- Subcontractor
- Owner
- Architect
- Florida Board of Insurance

Contractors must send a notice of all demolition projects to Florida Dept. of Environmental Protection ____ working days before demolition, even if there is no asbestos containing material present.

- 10
- 15
- 5
- 30

The check register shows at a glance _____.

- what expense categories you have and where your money goes.
- your income and expense items by category.
- your available balance on a cash basis.
- the income, expenses, and equity of your company.

When estimating speeds of equipment on the streets, they will usually average _____ of the speed limit.

- 70 – 80 percent
- 70 – 75 percent
- 40 – 65 percent
- 100 percent

Unless otherwise required in the Bidding Documents, the Agreement for the Work will be written on AIA Document _____, Standard Form of Agreement Between Owner and Contractor.

- A201
- A401
- A701
- A101

A _____ would be required to carry Liability and Property insurance in the respective amounts of $300,000 and $50,000.

- Pollutant Storage System
- Pool Contractor
- General Contractor
- Plumbing Contractor

Which of the following is a valid oral contract?

- two year apartment rental agreement
- agreement to buy a lawnmower for $475.00
- agreement to buy 3 pallets of bricks for $515.00
- all of the above

The Current Ratio gives a good idea of _____.

- a company's general financial strength
- a company's ability to meet current obligations with current assets
- a company's collection processes
- a debt to profit comparison

A fictitious name must be renewed every _____.

- year
- 2 years
- 5 years
- 7 years

If the Contractor defaults, or neglects to carry out the Work in accordance with the Contract Documents and fails within a _____ period after receipt of written notice from the Owner to commence and correction of such default or neglect with diligence and promptness… the Owner may correct such deficiencies..

- three day
- five day
- ten day
- fifteen day

A purchase order form will help you control _____.

- inventory sales
- your payment terms
- actual inventory in a LIFO system
- unauthorized purchases

Interpretations, corrections, and changes of the Bidding Documents will be made by _____.

- Addendum
- the Architect
- Change Order
- the Owner

The Department shall impose a special fee of $5.00 to _____.

- offset inflation
- cover increased legal fees and court expenses
- combat unlicensed activity
- to increase the social media availability of the CILB

If the Contractor does not pay the Subcontractor through no fault of the Subcontractor, within seven days of the time payment should be made as provided in this Agreement, the Subcontractor may, upon _____ additional days written notice to the Contractor, stop the Work of the Subcontract.

- 14
- 7
- 5
- 3

A company's financial year might be referred to as a(n) _____.

- fiscal year
- federal tax period
- accounting year
- year of the mule

Per AIA-A401, periodic progress reports on the Work shall be provided by the _____ to the _____.

- Contractor, Owner
- Contractor, Architect
- Subcontractor, Owner
- Subcontractor, Contractor

For Workers Compensation, _____ is *not* exempt from being considered a construction job.

- Landscaping for existing buildings
- Fencing for existing building
- Swimming pool repairs at an existing building
- Well drilling on land containing existing buildings

_____ is (are) considered to be a variable expense.

- Postage
- Rent
- Depreciation
- Collections

The Bidder shall provide Performance Bonds and Payment Bonds _____.

- in the amount of the Contract sum
- in the amount of the full cost of the job
- prior to the completion of the work
- only for jobs over $250,000 in cost

_____ insurance covers the structure being constructed and may be extended to cover materials while in transit or at temporary storage facilities.

- Umbrella
- Inland marine
- Fidelity
- Builders risk

If not exempt, the _____ will pay the sales tax.

- manufacturer
- state
- purchaser
- licensee

A loan for $150,000 is made at a 9% interest rate. It is paid back after 6 months. _____ in interest will be paid.

    $15,000
    $13,500
    $6,750
    $10,125

Bad Debts should be adjusted for in _____.

    accounts receivable
    accounts payable
    only cash basis accounting
    December of each year

If a contractor becomes liable for the payment of compensation to the employees of a subcontractor who has failed to secure such payment in violation of §440, the contractor shall be entitled to recover from the subcontractor _____.

    all benefits paid
    all benefits paid or payable plus interest
    150% of all benefits paid
    nothing

Under the Equal Pay Act, if the action is willful, a court or jury may award up to _____ back pay.

    three years
    two years
    two years, not to exceed $5,000
    two years, plus interest

83. The Contractor shall not contract with a proposed person or entity to whom _____ has made reasonable or timely objection.

    architect
    owner
    architect or owner
    architect or engineer

_____ may *not* be depreciated.

- a tractor
- a building
- equipment
- land

_____ must sign a Change Order.

- the owner
- the architect
- the owner and the architect
- the owner, the contractor, and the architect,

Contractor's claims for the cost of services or materials provided due to the Subcontractor's failure to execute the Work shall require ____ days written notice prior to the Contractor's providing services or materials.

- 2
- 3
- 5
- 7

A secondary qualifier is never responsible for _____.

- obtaining permits
- safety on the jobsite
- financial matters having to do with his/her jobsite
- quality of the work done on his/her jobsite

According to AIA, _____ will *not* be allowed to be charged for when a construction change order is requested.

- Labor
- Rental cost of hand tools
- Rental cost of machinery
- Supplies

A contractor shall submit to the architect his application for payment _____ days prior to the date established in a contract for progress payments.

    3
    5
    7
    10

_____ is a method of improving cash flow

    Maintaining a high inventory
    Taking advantage of discounts
    Converting all cash sales to accounts receivable
    Paying off liabilities

A subcontractor has a "Standard Form of Agreement Between Contractor and Subcontractor" with the prime contractor on a project. The ONLY way the subcontractor can assign work on the subcontract is with the written _____.

    consent of the owner or architect
    consent of the contractor
    notification to the owner or architect
    notification to the contractor

_____ eligible for Small Business Association loans,

    All building contractors in the Unites States
    Only company presidents
    Applicants who cannot obtain a loan from local banks
    Applicants who are recommended by a local bank

A Notice of Commencement can be extended past one year _____.

    if it is written into the Notice of Commencement
    if the job proceeds past one year
    when there is an architectural change order
    never

According to AIA, the bidder making a bid represents that he or she _____.

    is familiar with local conditions under which the work is to be performed
    is making a bid contingent on standard codes and conditions
    will adjust accordingly if the bid is accepted as long as an addendum is made
    will provide specifications for all materials

A contractor receives payment from the owner of a construction project. The contractor shall pay the subcontractor each progress payment within _____.

  3 working days
  3 days (including Saturday and Sunday)
  5 working days
  7 working days

When a piece of equipment is sold, it necessary to book the transaction separate from regular sales because _____.

  it is treated as a variable expense
  it receives different tax treatment
  the transaction is not taxable
  the gains or losses must be used to adjust gross profits

A certificate holder or registrant must inform the Board, by mail, within _____ calendar days, of changes in any information required to be stated on the application for qualification of a business organization.

  30
  45
  60
  90

_____ is (are) examples of an accrual entry.

  depreciation and amortization entries
  entries to record payroll taxes
  entries to record automatic loan payments
  entries to record purchase of material stored at jobsite

To establish an hourly cost for a piece of equipment, the contractor needs to consider all of the following except the _____.

  estimated life of the equipment
  cost of the equipment, less salvage value
  replacement cost of the equipment
  estimated average hours of use

Failure of a certificate holder or registrant to apply for renewal of an active certificate at the time of biennial renewal shall cause the certificate to become _____.

    temporarily suspended
    permanently suspended
    voluntarily inactive
    delinquent

The quarterly Federal Tax Form 941 summarizes tax liability for the employer which includes _____.

    liability insurance
    federal income taxes withheld
    workers compensation insurance
    federal unemployment insurance tax

_____ summarizes the existing conditions of a business.

    the balance sheet
    the cash flow statement
    the income statement
    the statement of retained earnings

Having received the list of subcontractors, the architect immediately objects to the use of plumber X's company. The general contractor then proposes and uses plumber Y's company at a higher cost of $5,000. The general contractor is entitled to _____.

    nothing
    a time extension only
    $5,000 plus a proven time extension
    re-negotiate the contract with the owner

The term "lapping" refers to _____ taken from the business by moving outstanding balances from one customer account to another.

    cash
    equity
    liabilities
    receivables

_____ is required to file a construction claim of lien.

    permission from the owner
    a court order

C. a direct contract with the owner
D. the claim must be recorded with the clerk of the court

106. _____ ratios compare accounts on the balance sheet to accounts on the income statement.

A. quick assets
   combined
   income
   current

The Florida's Workers' Compensation Act is applicable to an employer in the construction industry who employs _____ or more full or part time employees.

1
2
3
10

_____ is a type of cost basis inventory valuation method which uses the current market value of material as it is used.

specific cost
first in-first out
last in-first out
cost-plus inflation

According Builder's Guide to Accounting, _____ is not used when calculating goods sold to average inventory ratio.

labor
materials purchased
all other direct costs
total monthly averages

According to AIA-A201, _____ does **NOT** require a written notice in order to file a claim for additional cost.

minor change in the work
work performed because of a concealed condition
damages caused by the architect
work performed because of an emergency endangering the owner's property

According to Builder's Guide to Accounting, all the following are generally found on an invoice except _____.

a description of materials
the sales price of the materials

C. the terms of the invoice
D. the balance of the customer's account

Current liabilities include the portion of long-term debt for equipment purchases that is payable within _____.

    30 days
    90 days
    180 days
    365 days

Gross sales less direct costs equals _____ .

    gross profit
    net profit
    income from operations
    net sales

Assets minus liabilities equals _____.

    net profit
    net worth
    gross sales
    gross profit

Upon initial signing of an agreement or contract with a home owner, a contractor must deliver a written statement explaining the construction industry recovery fund. This action applies to all repairs, renovations, or construction over _____ in value.

    $500
    $1,500
    $2,500
    $5,000

An owner may terminate Notice of Commencement by executing a Notice of Termination that contains all of the following except _____ which of the following.

    recording office document book and Page reference numbers and date of Notice of commencement
    two copies of a Notice Direct Contract
    statement that lienors have been paid in full
    statement specifying that notice applies to all real property subject to Notice of Commencement

According to Builder's Guide to Accounting, successful builders control their costs BEST at _____.

    at the end of each week

B. during each phase of the work
C. immediately prior to approving invoices
D. in bi-weekly meetings with the owner present

During the year, a firm used several independent contractors to perform various services. Each of these services involved payments in excess of $600 to the independent contractor performing the services. The independent contractors were not employees of the company. The company's responsibility for reporting the earnings of these contractors to the Internal Revenue Service (I.R.S.) is that _____ .

- the company must immediately file a Form W-4 for these independent contractors
- the company must file Form 1099-MISC to report total payments of $600 or more to these contractors
- the company must carry the contractors as employees and report their earnings along with the company's hourly or salaried personal
- the company has no responsibility. The independent contractors are responsible for reporting their earnings to the I.R.S.

When preparing financial statements, accruals are used to record _____ .

- lump sum payments
- income earned but not yet received
- cash transactions
- prepayments on a future contract

Any contractor who collects a deposit of more than 10% of the contract price for any repairs, renovations, or construction to residential real property must apply for a permit within _____ days of payment.

- 7
- 10
- 30
- 45

_____ would not require use of the straight percentage of completion method.

- jobs longer than two years in duration
- firms that require periodic, progressive recognition of profit from their jobs
- construction jobs producing revenue greater than $10 million
- jobs costing $1,000 - $5,000 which take approximately one week to complete

One of the most practical and useful cash controls available is _____ .

- a daily cash summary

B. a quarterly cash summary
C. a secure petty cash box
D. keeping petty cash receipts

According to Builder's Guide to Accounting, all the following are procedures included in the budget process except _____.

    analyzing the results
    consulting with your accountant
    preparing the budget
    taking action to control expenses

According to Builder's Guide to Accounting, the best way to control equipment costs is good_____.

    maintenance
    scheduling
    financing
    reports

In order to establish an hourly cost for a bulldozer for job allocations, the _____ following would **NOT** apply.

    cost of equipment less salvage value
    operating costs involving gas, oil, and accessories
    repairing and maintenance costs
    unpredictable job site conditions

According to AIA, adjustment of the contract sum using a change order must be established based on_____.

    an agreement between the owner, contractor and architect
    the unit prices as stated in the contract documents
    labor, material and equipment costs
    the architect's recommendation

When preparing a financial statement for a lender before applying for a loan, it is best to first_____.

    A. accumulate current assets to improve the cash position

B. reduce current liabilities
C. try to decrease the current ratio
D. try to increase the volume of business

Every certified and registered contractor must complete a minimum of _____ hours of continuing education during every two-year license cycle.

3
7
14
16

Under Florida Law, your failure to make sure that all contractors, subcontractors, and material suppliers are paid may result in you paying _____.

improper payments
twice
unrecoverable payments
non-essential payments

Bidders to whom an award of a contract is under consideration shall submit to the architect, upon request, a _____ AIA document stating the contractor's qualifications.

A701
A401
312 6
305

An owner and lender determine that a project will cost $2,000,000 to build. The loan is obtained for $1,180,000, with the owner supplying the difference in cash funding. This contribution is known as _____.

a project loan
equity
a second mortgage
a subordinated loan

132. A claim for a contract adjustment, due to the effects of concealed conditions, must be made within _____.

A. ten days after the first observance of the condition

B. twenty-one days after the first observance of the condition
C. ten days after the date the architect has seen the condition
D twenty-one days after the architect has given notice of the decision

The original contract documents include the owner-contractor agreement, the general, supplementary and other conditions, and _____.

- the owner's right to clean up
- drawings and specifications
- proposal requests
- subcontracts

When a construction company is applying for a loan, most banks require all the following items except for _____.

- a current balance sheet
- a current income statement
- last year's federal income tax return
- last year's state income tax return

Freight charges on material shipped to a job by the supplier are defined as a _____ cost.

- direct
- incidental
- indirect
- overhead

For payroll record keeping, it is suggested to _____.

- have duplicate time cards properly signed and dated
- list payroll checks in separate check registers
- give separate stubs only to employees paid overtime that pay period
- give your accountant the names and amounts of each check given to each employee

To convince a lender to extend a loan, a contractor must demonstrate that he or she _____.

- will not be under undue financial strain from the loan payments
- has the loan amount in an account
- has a proven track record for performing excellent work
- has a minimum current ratio of 3 to 1

When preparing a bid estimate, the rental cost of a temporary building for the duration of a project should be _____.

    listed under the supplementary general conditions section
    listed under the fixed overhead section
    allocated as a percentage cost to cover this item
    allocated as an hourly cost to cover this item

_____ is considered an intangible asset.

    cash
    patents
    fixed assets
    prepaid assets

When sales equal the total of fixed, sales expenses and direct costs, this is referred to as _____.

    cash flow
    available cash
    balance sheet
    breakeven point

Real turnover is an example of a (an) _____ ratio.

    combined
    current
    income
    expense

Deferred income should be entered on a balance sheet as a _____.

    current liability
    long term liability
    deferred credit
    current asset

The base penalty, before adjustments, for failure to post OSHA citations is _____.

- $2,000
- $3,000
- $5,000
- $7,000

The purpose of preparing an income statement is to _____.

- Borrow construction funds or secure personal credit
- Divide information into various categories to prepare the cash flow statement
- Show control of costs and expenses, the volume of business, and income yield
- Predict profits over a period of time

The unemployment compensation laws apply to any employer who has one or more employees, and either employed at least one employee for any portion of a day for 20 weeks in a calendar year, or paid _____.

- $400 in wages during any calendar week
- $600 in wages during any calendar month
- $1,000 in wages during any calendar quarter
- $1,500 in wages during any calendar quarter

_____ are required to be licensed under Florida Statutes Section 489.103.

- Persons who sell, service, or install heating or air conditioning units that have a capacity of less than 3 tons with a power cord
- Registered architects or engineers acting within the scope of their practice
- Persons performing small remodeling jobs with a contract price of less than $2,500
- Highway, street, road, bridge or railway contractors

Construction project schedules should have progress posted at least _____.

- Daily
- Weekly
- Biweekly

Monthly

An OSHA 300 safety log must be maintained by employers with at least _____ employees.

    5
    7
    10
    11

OSHA 300 Log on Summary of Occupational Injuries and Illnesses is used to record _____.

    Accident investigations
    All health claims
    All incidents resulting in loss of consciousness
    Non-work restricting injuries

_____ is an estimating method that is **NOT** recommended for lump sum contracts.

    approximate estimated method
    detailed survey method
    square footage method
    unit price method

When determining a project bid, the _____ is (are) considered to be an overhead expense.

    costs of recruiting laborers for that job
    materials needed for that job
    purchases of small tools
    rental of equipment to be used only for that job

A typical purchase order should include all of the following **EXCEPT** _____.

    the billing and delivery address
    a preprinted purchase order number
    sales tax for purchase and for resale
    an authorized signature

A definite plan for fixed assets should include all of the following **EXCEPT** _____.

A. records of maintenance cost
B. a determination if proposed equipment is useful for the job
C. a policy establishing depreciation rates
D. a study of lease vs. purchase options

You may not claim depreciation on any of the following **EXCEPT** _____.

   land
   inventory
   vehicles
   intangible property

Florida sales tax is _____.

   Reported on form DR-15-CS and paid on a monthly basis
   Reported on form DR-15-CS and paid on a quarterly basis
   Reported on form 941 and paid on a monthly basis
   Reported on form 941 and paid on a quarterly basis

Expanding a business usually requires a great deal of capital to purchase new equipment, buildings or to obtain long term financing. To qualify for expansion financing, financial institutes typically require that you have been in business at least _____, while _____ is preferred.

   2 years; 4 years
   2 years; 5 years
   3 years; 5 years
   3 years; 6 years

Final payment to the Subcontractor shall be made when the Work is completed and the _____ has issued a certificate of payment.

   Owner
   Contractor
   Inspector
   Architect

Regarding Worker's Compensation, a certificate of election to be exempt is valid for _____ after the effective date stated thereon.

   1 year
   2 years
   3 years

D. 5 years

*** Please see answer key on the following page***

Sample Practice Test
1 Exam Prep
Business and Finance
Simulated Practice Exam 2 – 125 Questions

ANSWER KEY

		Section /Page#	**Book**
1.	B	5-30	Florida Contractors Manual
2.	A	5-30	Florida Contractors Manual
3.	B	2-20	Florida Contractors Manual
4.	D	7-16	Florida Contractors Manual
5.	C	3-154	Florida Contractors Manual
6.	A	455.217(4) / 2-38	Florida Contractors Manual
7.	D	5-58	Florida Contractors Manual
8.	B	13.4.1, 13.4.3	AIA Document A201
9.	D	5-32	Florida Contractors Manual
10.	C	87	Builder's Guide to Accounting

$39,000 + $91,000 = $125,000 (cost to date + cost to complete = total cost)
$125,000 x .12 (12%) = $15,000 add for profit
$125,000 + $15,000 = $140,000 total contract

11.	A	5-15, 5-19, 5-16	Florida Contractors Manual
12.	D	455.273 / 2-55	Florida Contractors Manual
13.	B	5-17	Florida Contractors Manual

		Section /Page#	**Book**
14.	C	10-88	Florida Contractors Manual
15.	D	5-19	Florida Contractors Manual
16.	C	5-49	Florida Contractors Manual
17.	A	455.214 (2) / 2-36	Florida Contractors Manual
18.	C	7-6	Florida Contractors Manual
19.	C	455.243 / 2-53	Florida Contractors Manual
20.	D	455.218 (1)(a) / 2-40	Florida Contractors Manal
21.	B	455.213 (6) / 2-35	Florida Contractors Manual
22.	A	271	Builder's Guide to Accounting
23.	D	455.214 (2) / 2-36	Florida Contractors Manual
24.	C	455.214 (1) / 2-36	Florida Contractors Manual
25.	B	455.2175 / 2-38	Florida Contractors Manual
26.	C	10-31, 10.32 - Figure 12	Florida Contractors Manual
27.	A	163-164	Builder's Guide to Accounting

Purchase value minus salvage value: $210,000 - $30,000 = $180,000

Note: when calculation depreciation with salvage value, always subtract salvage value from purchase price before starting calculations.

This value is used to determine annual depreciation (12) years: $180,000 ÷ 12 = $15,000 per year

Total depreciation after 6 years: $15,000 x 6 = $90,000

#	Ans	Section /Page#	Book
28.	B	7.2.1	AIA A701
29.	B	59	Builder's Guide to Accounting
30.	C	5-11	Florida Contractors Manual
31.	A	6-5	Florida Contractors Manual
32.	B	10-63	Florida Contractors Manual
33.	C	2-24	Florida Contractors Manual
34.	D	7-6	Florida Contractors Manual
35.	D	3.2.2	AIA Document A701
36.	A	3-12	Florida Contractors Manual

Assets = Liabilities + Equity - therefore, Assets – Liabilities = Equity

#	Ans	Section /Page#	Book
37.	C	10-2	Florida Contractors Manual
38.	D	4-15	Florida Contractors Manual
39.	A	1-23	Florida Contractors Manual
40.	B	1-18	Florida Contractors Manual
41.	C	5-292	Florida Contractors Manual
42.	C	1-12	Florida Contractors Manual

43.	D	1-15	Florida Contractors Manual
44.	D	5-14	Florida Contractors Manual
45.	B	7-16	Florida Contractors Manual
46.	A	2.4	AIA Document A201
		Section /Page#	**Book**
47.	A	208	Builder's Guide to Accounting
48.	C	7-6	Florida Contractors Manual
49.	B	163	Builder's Guide to Accounting

$157,000 \div 7 = 22.500

50.	B	10-67	Florida Contractors Manual
51.	C	3-80	Florida Contractors Manual
52.	D	7.2.1	AIA Document A201
53.	A	23	Builder's Guide to Accounting

$210,000 + $105,000 = $315,000. $210,000 \div $315,000 = .667 (66.67\%)$

54.	C	23	Builder's Guide to Accounting

Apply percentage complete to contract price - $.6667 x $390,000 = $260,013

55.	B	23	Builder's Guide to Accounting

Paid $220,000   Earned $260,013

56.	B	5-15	Florida Contractors Manual
57.	A	10-72	Florida Contractors Manual
58.	B	11.1.4	AIA Document A201
59.	A	10-97	Florida Contractors Manual
60.	A	101	Builder's Guide to Accounting

#	Ans	Section /Page#	Book
61.	C	10-27	Florida Contractors Manual
62.	D	8.1.1	AIA Document A701
63.	C	2-157	Florida Contractors Manual
64.	B	8-6	Florida Contractors Manual
65.	B	269	Builder's Guide to Accounting
66.	C	1-14	Florida Contractors Manual
67.	C	2.5	AIA Document A201
68.	D	116	Builder's Guide to Accounting
69.	A	3.2.3	AIA Document A701
70.	C	455.2281 / 2-51	Florida Contractors Manual
71.	B	4.7	AIA Document A401
72.	A	3-31	Florida Contractors Manual
73.	D	4.1.4	AIA Document A401
74.	C	6-6	Florida Contractors Manual
75.	D	142	Builder's Guide to Accounting
76.	A	7.2.2	AIA Document A201
77.	D	4-7	Florida Contractors Manual
78.	C	3-64	Florida Contractors Manual
79.	C	3-74	Florida Contractors Manual

$150,0000 x .09 (9%) x 6 months/12 months in a year = $6,750

80.	A	64	Builder's Guide to Accounting
81.	B	440.10 (d)1 / 6-92	Florida Contractors Manual
82.	A	5-39	Florida Contractors Manual
		Section /Page#	**Book**
83.	C	5.2.2	AIA Document A201
84.	D	162	Builder's Guide to Accounting
85.	D	7.2.1	AIA Document A201
86.	D	3.3.2.1	AIA Document A401
87.	C	2-21	Florida Contractors Manual
88.	B	7.3.7.3	AIA Document A201
89.	D	9.3.1	AIA Document A201
90.	B	262	Builder's Guide to Accounting
91.	B	7.4.2	AIA Document A401
92.	C	318, 319	Builder's Guide to Accounting
93.	A	713.13 (1)(c) / 9-88	Florida Contractors Manual
94.	A	2.1.3	AIA Document A701
95.	D	11.3	AIA Document A401
96.	B	170	Builder's Guide to Accounting
97.	B	61G4-15.007 / 2-159	Florida Contractors Manual

98.	D	237	Builder's Guide to Accounting
99.	C	159, 160	Builder's Guide to Accounting
100.	D	489.116(4) / 2-84	Florida Contractors Manual
101.	B	137, 138	Builder's Guide to Accounting
		Section /Page#	**Book**
102	A	247	Builder's Guide to Accounting
103.	C	5.2.3	AIA Document A201
104.	A	181	Builder's Guide to Accounting
105.	D	713.08(5) / 9-84	Florida Contractors Manual
106.	B	270	Builder's Guide to Accounting
107.	A	6-5	Florida Contractors Manual
108.	C	120	Builder's Guide to Accounting
109.	D	121	Builder's Guide to Accounting
110.	D	Section 4.3.5	AIA Document A201
111.	D	44 / Figure 3-6	Builder's Guide to Accounting
112.	D	155	Builder's Guide to Accounting
113.	A	248	Builder's Guide to Accounting
114.	B	247	Builder's Guide to Accounting
115.	C	489.1425 / 2-105	Florida Contractors Manual
116.	B	713.132(1) / 9-91	Florida Contractors Manual

#	Ans	Section/Page#	Book
117.	B	189	Builder's Guide to Accounting
118.	B	138	Builder's Guide to Accounting
119.	B	106, 107	Builder's Guide to Accounting
120.	C	489.126(2) / 2-90	Florida Contractors Manual
		Section /Page#	**Book**
121.	D	25	Builder's Guide to Accounting
122.	A	180	Builder's Guide to Accounting
123.	B	144	Builder's Guide to Accounting
124.	B	228	Builder's Guide to Accounting
125.	D	159, 160	Builder's Guide to Accounting
126.	A	7.1.1	AIA Document A701
127.	B	174	Builder's Guide to Accounting
128.	C	489.115(4)(a) / 2-82	Florida Contractors Manual
129.	B	713.06(2)(c) / 9-76	Florida Contractors Manual
130.	D	6.1	AIA Document A701
131.	B	3-84	Florida Contractors Manual
132.	D	4.3.4	AIA Document A201
133.	B	1.1.1	AIA Document A201
134.	D	317	Builder's Guide to Accounting
135.	A	115	Builder's Guide to Accounting

#	Ans	Section /Page#	Book
136.	B	126	Builder's Guide to Accounting
137.	A	316	Builder's Guide to Accounting
138.	A	10-11, 10-14	Florida Contractors Manual
139.	B	253	Builder's Guide to Accounting
		Section /Page#	**Book**
140.	D	179	Builder's Guide to Accounting
141.	A	273	Builder's Guide to Accounting
142.	C	191	Builder's Guide to Accounting
143.	B	7-32	Florida Contractor Manual
144.	C	249	Builder's Guide to Accounting
145.	D	5-277	Florida Contractor Manual
146.	C	489.103(9) / 2-66, 2-67	Florida Contractor Manual
147.	B	10-63	Florida Contractor Manual
148.	D	7-9	Florida Contractor Manual
149.	C	7-19	Florida Contractor Manual
150.	C	10-12	Florida Contractor Manual
151.	C	142, 143	Builder's Guide to Accounting
152.	C	116, 117	Builder's Guide to Accounting
153.	B	156	Builder's Guide to Accounting
154.	C	162	Builder's Guide to Accounting

155.	A	1-23	Florida Contractor Manual
156.	B	3-72	Florida Contractor Manual
157.	D	11.3.1	AIA Document A401
158.	B	440.05(6) / 6-82	Florida Contractor Manual

Made in United States
Orlando, FL
04 October 2023

37564096R00148